MATT RUDNITSKY

You Are an Author

So Write Your F*cking Book

Contents

Knock, Knock   vi

Don't Listen To Me   viii

Experts Are Insecure Fools   1

Wait, Anyone Can Be A Writer?   5

Why Blogging Sucks   8

It's Impossible To Get Published   11

Publishers Are Dead   14

Everyone Is Dying   21

Self Publishing Is Easy As Instagram   23

Wait, The Martian Was Self-Published?   25

Writers Can Get Rich (Indirectly)   29

But, But, But!   33

But Buts Lie   34

But I Don't Have Enough to Say   39

But I'm Not An "Expert" (Dry Heave)   45

But Is It Worth Your Time?   47

But You Have Nothing To Lose   50

The One True But   56

Step 1: Treat Your Book Like A Startup   62

Step 2: Spy On Your Readers   64

Step 3: Steal Readers   68

Bonus: You're Building Your Publishing Muscle   75

Step 4: Make Your Readers Friends   77

Step 5: Realize Your Non-Expertise Is Your Advantage   83

Step 6: Paint Your Idea Purple   91

Step 7: Spell Out Your Thesis   92

Aside: For Fiction, Memoir And Books Without ROI   96

Step 8: Tell People Not To Read Your Book   98

Step 9: Outline Non-Anally   105

Step 10: More Research!   111

Step 11: Get Scared   113

Step 12: Chill   115

Step 13: Make Writing A Habit   118

Step 14: Find Your Triggers   122

Step 15: Treat Yourself Like A Baby   128

Step 16: What Is "Writing," Anyway?   136

Step 17: F*ck Friction   139

Step 18: Treat Yo'self   141

Step 19: Get Accountable   143

Habit Recap   145

Step 20: STOP!   147

Step 21: Write Drunk   150

Step 22: Edit Sober   153

Step 23: Fuck Around   157

Step 24: Give Up   159

Step 25: Focus On Word Of Mouth   162

Step 26: Put In The Batteries   168

Step 27: Follow The Sexy Book Recipe   171

Step 28: Get Emails In Your Book!   179

Step 29: Get Feedback   181

Aside: Editors   183

Step 30: Soft Launch   185

Step 31: Publish Your F*cking Book   188

Step 32: Give It Away   190

Step 33: Anti-Launch   194

Step 34: Relax About FOMO   197

Step 35: Ignore Sales   200

Step 36: Fucking Enjoy It   201
Step 37: Move On   202
Learn More   204

Knock, Knock

"You can write whatever the fuck you want in a self-published book." - Confucius' Daughter, Joelle

I'm Matt Rudnitsky, and I went from unemployed, 22-year-old idiot, to guy who self-published a book, *Smart Sports Betting*, that made $1,150.06 in profits its second month and over $14,000 total, as of this writing. Despite being an Economics major, despite being a "math and science person," despite doing zero "marketing" and despite putting zero effort into promotion post-launch.

Royalties Earned (What's this?) ▾

Currency	eBook Royalty	Paperback Royalty	KU/KOLL Royalty	Total Royalty
USD	3,844.91	9,591.87	569.13	14,005.91
GBP	109.61	117.75	18.38	245.74
EUR	58.00	101.19	9.56	168.75
JPY	967.00	0.00	16.53	983.53
INR	223.20	0.00	99.58	322.78
CAD	181.84	0.00	18.50	200.34
BRL	47.42	0.00	10.20	57.62
MXN	6.86	0.00	16.01	22.87
AUD	132.31	0.00	6.72	139.03

Generate Report (What's this?) ▾

I spent $5 total on publishing and promoting the book.

I've completely ignored the book for 21 months, and yet I make money daily.

The book also helped me become a professional writer and editor. I've self-published two more books, edited and marketed a handful—and I write other people's books as a Scribe and Writer for Tucker Max's thriving startup, Scribe. I've gotten a variety of freelance copywriting, editing and other writing jobs, in large part due to the indirect value of my book. I work remotely, so I'm traveling the world, writing in cafes and co-working spaces. Right now, I'm in Lisbon. Next month, Rabat, Morocco.

Writing a book will change your life.

I'm not trying to impress you. I'm a decent writer; that's all.

My point is: If *I* can make a living writing, anyone can. When I started, I was just some 22-year-old, unemployed idiot.

My writing career started with that self-published book. A book can be the platform off which you build a writing career or business, or it can take your existing career or business to the next level, acting as a business card on steroids.

If I can write successful books and become a writer who doesn't starve, anyone can.

It's your turn, and all you need to do is read the following words, written by an idiot who stumbled into mild success.

You know you have a book in you. You know you are an author. You just have to get that book out and between two covers.

Don't Listen To Me

"When you're trying to create a career as a writer, a little delusional thinking goes a long way." - Michael Lewis

I have a story that might be valuable to you. I believe I can share my failures and successes so you can save time, but remember: Writing books is art. So is life.

My way worked for me, but it's not the only way.

Ask questions. Experiment. There are no wrong questions, and there are no wrong answers.

You can always email me at info@plat.pub for help. There's no such thing as a stupid question, just insecure assholes unaware that the more questions you ask, the more you learn.

1

Experts Are Insecure Fools

"She generally gave herself very good advice, (though she very seldom followed it), and sometimes she scolded herself so severely as to bring tears into her eyes; and once she remembered trying to box her own ears for having cheated herself in a game of croquet she was playing against herself, for this curious child was very fond of pretending to be two people. 'But it's no use now,' thought poor Alice, 'to pretend to be two people! Why, there's hardly enough of me left to make one *respectable person!'* " - Lewis Carroll, Alice's Adventures in Wonderland

It all started when I realized my high school guidance counselor didn't know what the hell she was talking about.

I always did well in school, because I thought you *had to*. Grades equaled success, which equaled money, which equaled happiness.

I was realistic. At seven, I'd given up on playing for the Yankees. At 14, I'd given up on General Managing the Yankees. At 17, I'd given up on being an agent for Yankees players.

I'm writing this from London, where, fittingly, people insult me by calling me a Yankee.

"I guess I could major in business?" I told my guidance counselor, handing her the list my parents and I had carefully made, containing 14 excellent, fun schools with good business programs.

"This is a good list of *reach*es," she told me, the kid with a 100.3 GPA. I was confused. They weren't Ivy League schools.

"Let me look at your transcript ...

... hm, you're doing best in AP Physics, how about engineering?"

Engineering didn't appeal to me. I had earned 100% in AP Physics, because it was graded on a curve. My math and science and English grades were also A+. "I don't think..." She interrupted me.

"I'll find some good engineering programs," she told the kid who was trying to tell her he didn't want to be a fucking engineer.

She typed and typed and handed me a sheet of paper with 50+ colleges on it. She had visited some database, typed in "SCHOOLS THAT HAVE ENGINEERING," with maybe one more filter, and gave me the least helpful list in the history of lists.

I went to a "good" high school in white suburbia, and I was one of the "best" students in my class.

"Good luck!" Our meeting was over.

Implied: *I wouldn't get into my desired schools.* (I did.)

I should be an engineer. (I'm now a writer.)

She knew what she was good for me. (She didn't.)

I sat silently as my blood boiled, trying to keep a neutral face, but all I could think was, *I worked my ass of for 13 years, for this?*

I realized most of the *should*s in my life were coming from insecure people who couldn't back up their opinions, and only cared about keeping their jobs.

My guidance counselor was recognized as an "expert," but didn't want me getting rejected from schools, getting mad and ruining her reputation. She couldn't back up her credential with real value.

Her incentives didn't line up with mine, and neither did her morals.

I got into almost every school, and was told I *should* major in something "practical." Nobody could tell me why Economics, where we studied a "perfect free market economy in which all actors are rational," when people were so clearly *not*, then a bunch of calculus, was "practical." But I listened, because I was told I *should*.

Economics, as taught in school, was not "practical." The degree existed to impress people. I *should* have majored in something I actually enjoyed.

That was the last straw.

Whenever someone said or implied I *should* do something, I asked a string of *whys*, until I was content.

It's like when your parents told you you *should* do your homework after school. *Why?*

Because you're supposed to.

Why?

Because you need to get good grades.

Why?

Because you need to get into a good college.

Why?

Because you need to get into a good college to get a good job.

What's a good job? Am I guaranteed to get one if I get into a good college? Why is everyone who has a "good job" miserable? Why are there lots of people who didn't go to college who are happy?

It was all a sham. The *should*s were merely suggestions, and they were usually shitty suggestions.

Don't even get me started on *can't*s.

You *can't* write a book, unless you were an English major wordsmith, with an MFA, who has an agent, and has toiled away in cafes for years, and has fourteen unpublished novels in his drawer.

I floated by in college, drinking and playing video games, cynical and angry at all the insecure "experts" who had told me I *should* aspire to be an unhappy cog in an inefficient machine.

I knew what I *didn't* want to do, but I didn't yet know what the hell I *did* want to do.

As always, the answer came by drunkenly stumbling forwards. Key word: *forwards.*

2

Wait, Anyone Can Be A Writer?

" 'Why is it,' Jonathan puzzled, 'that the hardest thing in the world is to convince a bird that he is free, and that he can prove it for himself if he'd just spend a little time practicing? Why should that be so hard?' Fletcher still blinked from the change of scene. 'What did you just do? How did we get here?' 'You did say you wanted to be out of the mob, didn't you?' 'Yes! But how did you...' 'Like everything else, Fletcher. Practice.' - Richard Bach, Jonathan Livingston Seagull

Majoring in Economics sucked, and I liked sports, so I asked about joining the sports section of Michigan's student newspaper.

"Just show up to a meeting," they told the clueless freshman. Really? They all knew each other and had inside jokes and I was scared. They were writers, and I wasn't. I didn't belong. I'd just observe.

Before writing an article, you shadow someone. After college, my shadow got hired by the *New York Times*. At the time, he covered the Michigan hockey team, coached by legend Red Berenson, the world's

5

most intimidating 69-year-old. Berenson still skated with the team, daily. "Wait there," he barked, as we sat in his office's waiting room, in historic Yost Arena.

I observed the interview silently, trying not to wet myself.

Next meeting, I still trembled, still an impostor, observing the writers do *their* thing. We weren't the same species. I was a fly on the wall; they were smart, accomplished humans. Flies can't become humans.

Anyone want to cover men's tennis? We had a highly-ranked tennis team, the nation's top freshman, and tennis was my favorite sport. My hand was anchored by fear (or perhaps gravity). Nobody moved. *Anyone?* Somehow my hand raised. Put it down! Too late.

It was an away match; I had to interview the coach and a player on the phone. I asked nervous, generic questions. *What did you think about the team's performance?* I transcribed the recording, and wrote the article in two days. It was decent.

They hadn't yet taught me the publishing protocol. I emailed my article to the Sports Editor.

"The deadline was 11pm the night of the match. Two days ago."

I had a two-hour deadline. The article took me 20. My writing career had ended before getting published once.

But the editor was nice and insisted I try again the following week.

I sweated and cringed and was sure my article sucked, but I finished. I learned Parkinson's Law. "Work expands so as to fill the time available for its completion." It's not bullshit; it's behavioral psychology.

Note to self: Deadlines are essential. You can do more than you think, quicker than you think. My first article was fine.

My name was in Ann Arbor's only daily newspaper. Technically, I was a writer.

But I didn't feel like one. I had broken some law and infiltrated a society of people better than me. Flies can't become humans. I would be exposed any day, and people would laugh and stab me with their favorite brand of pen, and write about it to universal praise. *Non-writer pretends he's a writer, stabbed with Pilot G-2, murderer rewarded with book deal.*

For some reason, they let me cover the tennis team. I improved, got an online sportswriting internship, kept writing, and people kept calling me a *writer.* Even though I was an Econ major, always told he was a "math and science guy."

Becoming a writer is simple. All you do is write things and publish them under your name.

Weird.

Stupid, maybe.

But wasn't that how all writers became writers? Hemingway and Co. didn't take a test, or get a degree or certificate. Bukowski worked in a post office. Majoring in English doesn't make you a writer. Getting an MFA is difficult, of questionable value, and still doesn't make you a writer.

To be a writer, you need to publish something in public. If you haven't done that, do it. Now you're a writer, too. The club isn't secret. There's open membership.

I wrote things and published them under my name, so I put "writer" on my resume. I could dress it up with bullshit jargon. *Staff writer for Ann Arbor's only daily, independent newspaper, covering NCAA's 15th-ranked men's varsity tennis team.*

I'm not trying to impress you. My point is: If I can be a writer, *anyone* can be a writer.

I had always ranted to my friends about sports. Turned out, I just had to publish those rants to become a writer.

Still, I thought it would be decades 'til I could write a *book.*

I *should* wait 'til I'm ready.

As usual, I was wrong. Idiot.

3

Why Blogging Sucks

"Men are anxious to improve their circumstances, but are unwilling to improve themselves; they therefore remain bound." - James Allen, As a Man Thinketh

Somehow, I stumbled into becoming a full-time editor and writer at a national sports blog, SportsGrid. I wrote an average of seven 600-word articles a day, for over two years.

I thought writing thousands of words a day was an impossible joke, but when the alternative was getting fired, I got used to it quickly. *Parkinson's Law.*

But my most popular articles were irrelevant within days, if not minutes. One of my best articles caused its subject, a felon, to call my mother and threaten to "slit my throat," but even *he* stopped bothering me after two months.

The news is heroin's nonlethal cousin.

Blog, CLICKS! GET HIGH!, no one cares ... blog, CLICKS! GET HIGH!, no one cares, I feel like shit, BUT WANT MORE, but when does the cycle end?

4,200 words per day, 250 working days per year, plus a summer. Shit. I was good at math once. I must have written about ... 2,478,000 words. Millions of words produced, tethered to a computer, unable to leave between the hours of 9 and 5, making shit money, watching the value of those words vanish minutes after publishing.

Fuck.

I thought avoiding the corporate world had been smart, but I was doing the same thing in the blogosphere, for a third of the salary.

My words were just sitting there in Internet purgatory, read by no one, entertaining no one, making no money.

They started as mildly valuable, but shrunk to useless in minutes.

My poor words. I had worked so hard to extract them from my idiot brain.

I was a starving blogger. Ramen Noodles. No recognition. When I told people I was a sports blogger, they'd go, "Cool. So what do you do for money?"

Offensive, but accurate.

So I quit and moved to Prague, to live in a $350 a month apartment and teach English to 4-year olds who didn't know how to say "hello."

It was a small, picturesque Czech village called Říčany . Then one of my 34 toddlers' teeth got punched out, by accident, so, *Czech this out*, his mom berated me.

*What are you going to **do** about it!* She yelled and waved her arms like those used car dealer marshmallow balloon things. I had already cleaned and consoled him, but I couldn't watch 34 toddlers at once.

The pay was shit, so I quit.

I remembered those *two and a half million words* I had written.

My (short, nonfiction) book would eventually be 25,000 words.

2,478,000 words could have filled *ninety-nine short books*.

Obviously, I wouldn't have written 99 books in two years. But I could've written a couple, at least.

It was like investing in a stock that had a guaranteed ROI of zero. My words cost time and sweat, yet had zero future value.

I had no income. I had to do *something*.

Most writers ignore sports betting because it's taboo, and technically illegal. I wrote about it regularly, and while the number of clicks wasn't as high as my more clickbait-y stuff, I had a small group of engaged readers: Tweeting, emailing, asking questions.

What if I wrote a book about sports betting?

I told a few friends. They thought it was cute. Maybe one day, they said.

Idiot me listened. At first.

4

It's Impossible To Get Published

"I know that we've been screwed royally ... all of us. But to spend my time more on that old story? I'd rather spend my time on the solution. Every great person I know spends 1% of their time on the problem, 99% of their time on the solution." - Tony Robbins, Money: Master The Game

Y ou want to *get published*, so you can *become an author*, and *write a bestseller*, so people will read your words or buy your product or service. That means you need a publisher to accept you. Probably after getting an agent to accept you.

There was no way I was "getting published" as a 22-year old, unemployed ex-sports blogger.

Turns out, it's almost impossible even if you're a great writer.

Publishers said Dr. Seuss was "too different from other juveniles on the market to warrant its selling." He has sold over 300 million copies, the 9th-best-selling fiction author of all-time. I'd let that genius doctor deliver my child.

Chicken Soup for the Soul was rejected 144 times. "Anthologies don't sell," they said. 125 million sales.

The Da Vinci Code: "It is so badly written." 80 million sales.

Vladimir Nabakov's *Lolita*, widely considered one of history's greatest novels, was rejected by all major publishers. "I recommend it be buried under a stone for a thousand years." He had to flee to France to get it published. 50 million sales.

The War of the Worlds was "an endless nightmare."

Robert Pirsig's *Zen and the Art of Motorcycle Maintenence* was rejected by 121 publishers. It's my favorite book and a "cultural icon in literature."

So you're supposed to beg pretentious publishers to accept you, but they probably won't, and even if they do, *the readers are still the ones who decide if your book is good?*

Publishers aren't incentivized to take risks. If they copy what has worked in the past, working with established authors or dumbed-down, copycat templates, they know they'll do OK.

When you hold the keys to the gate, and people are begging to get in: your incentive is simply to not screw up. You're not trying to maximize profits, and you won't take chances. You have power, and you don't want to lose it. Just don't screw up so badly that your boss (or the market) takes the keys.

Like my guidance counselor. If she had gotten my hopes up and I had gotten rejected, I might have complained, and she might have gotten fired. Better to keep expectations low and meet them.

That's why sports coaches tend to be ultra-conservative. They punt on 4th-and-1 when they should go for it, because while success would be rewarding, failure would be *obvious*.

Our culture rewards risk-takers, but only when they win. And our culture doesn't punish people for opting not to act. **We ostracize people for wrong actions, but we barely notice inaction.** And we forget it quickly, because the results are hidden.

A lost bet makes you look bad and can get you fired, even if you took a calculated risk. Opting to play it safe means you won't look stupid in the moment.

This is why Hollywood dumbs things down. They're content to hit double after double, rather than go for a home run, but risk striking out.

There's this idea that publishers know what readers want. It's bullshit. They make safe bets, and keep the original stuff from readers.

It's not their fault. They're responding to incentives like all humans.

If you have power and you take a risk, you risk looking stupid, and having your power weakened.

How many people have never tried to "get published," because it was too intimidating, or not worth their time?

I didn't bother. Publishers would have laughed at me, a 22-year old, unemployed nobody.

The beautiful thing about being an unemployed nobody, though, is you have nothing to lose.

5

Publishers Are Dead

"Books and ideas are antifragile and get nourishment from attacks." - Nassim Taleb, Antifragile

When I visited Moscow, I saw Vladimir Lenin's embalmed corpse. Creepy.

My 19 fellow Americans and I put our phones in a bin and followed scary Russian soldiers inside. We descended stairs into a cavernous basement and walked in a single-file line, breathing in the cold, dark air.

We'd walk a minute, hit a corner, and meet a stoic soldier clutching his rifle, wearing that stereotypical Russian scowl, unflinching. Another corner, another soldier. Clearly designed to make our heart tremble. It worked.

We circled the halls like obedient elementary school kids, not daring to break the rules and speak.

We reached Lenin, propped up in a coffin, lifelike. Like a quality wax museum figurine, surrounded by an aura of creepy gravitas. You couldn't help but stare and shiver and think this man was important and powerful. That you should revere and fear him.

We all trembled as if this man was alive and judging our every move and we were not worthy.

That's what it's like to be a writer.

You know you have potential. You know that you have something to say. But it's so damn intimidating. You need the big, bad publishers or magazine editors or whomever to accept you, and even if they do, you'll still struggle to make a living. You feel egotistical putting your writing out there, as if you *know* people care about your thoughts, without anyone asking for them. That's why you want approval from a publisher. I felt the same way.

Then I got my phone back and saw sunlight and spoke with my friends. I felt normal, despite being in Russia. I realized: Lenin was just a waxy corpse. Was it even his real body? Can you preserve a body that long?

Publishing companies are waxy corpses. Like my guidance counselor, like Enbalmed Lenin.

Formerly powerful. Might still *look* powerful and scare you. People discuss and praise their power. But they're actually useless and dead.

It's hard to "get published." It's also useless.

A book's success is determined by what readers think. Publishers' opinions are irrelevant.

In the past, you needed a permission slip to sell to readers, so they could then decide. That permission slip was hard to get.

Now, you can reach readers directly, without a permission slip. Publishers don't have to sign off. They're waxy corpse Hall Monitors, and flash their badges so that you think you need their permission. But you can just walk around them, self-publish, and they can't do anything about it.

Publishers had four advantages in the past, but they're all gone, thanks to technology.

1) Distribution.

You used to need publishers to get you into bookstores. How would anyone find your book?

Now, anyone can publish any book on Amazon, for free. Amazon is a virtual bookstore, where about half of all book sales occur. Amazon is the world's biggest search engine for product searches. Yes, above Google.

You don't need to be in a bookstore anymore, and if your book does well online, you'll be able to get into bookstores later on, anyway.

2) Printing.

It used to be expensive to print books, so you needed a publisher to act as an investor and foot your bill. They tended to be very conservative and risk-averse. It was easier to invest in proven concepts (proven authors, boilerplate plots, etc.), because original work had a more uncertain return on investment.

Because publishers controlled distribution (bookstore placement) and production (printing), you used to need them. Now, they don't control either.

Companies like CreateSpace (affiliated with Amazon) can **print on demand.** When someone orders your book, CreateSpace can print a paperback version so quickly and cheaply that the reader can receive it the next day.

This means they don't need to hold any inventory, so they have zero risk in accepting your book to be published.

In the past, publishers would only print a book that they thought had a high chance of selling. They didn't want to be stuck with extra inventory.

Now, CreateSpace doesn't have to guess how many copies your book can sell, so they can take on virtually unlimited books. "Print runs" are no longer necessary.

This is revolutionary.

There is zero risk for CreateSpace to accept your book. If I wrote a book titled "Matt is cool! by Matt," that contained the sentence "Matt is cool haha lol" and a bunch of blank pages, *CreateSpace would accept it.*

If my mother bought it, CreateSpace would make a couple bucks, and so would I. They print zero advance copies, so it costs them nothing to publish your book, and it costs you nothing to "get published."

If nobody buys your book, they lose zero money, and you paid nothing beyond your time.

If one person buys it, they make a tiny sum, and so do you.

If many people buy it, they make a lot, and so do you.

Risk-free on both sides, and win-win.

3) Making it look good/professional.

People don't buy books that don't look professional. It signals haphazard work. Books should be polished.

For that, you need quality editing and cover and interior design, and social proof (blurbs and reviews).

Publishers can provide all of those things.

But in the new economy, you can often get better quality work for cheaper by using freelancers online. (Upwork, 99 designs, independent designers, etc.) And as I'll explain, you won't need to spend a dollar until your book is proven. You can get a "good enough" book published for free, and you can make it better, later, if it makes enough money to pay for the upgrades.

Some self-published authors don't bother making a paperback version, but nearly 75% of my profits have come from paperback sales. Don't make that mistake. Use CreateSpace.

4) Marketing (Discovery).

Before social media (Facebook, Goodreads, etc), email, blogs, podcasts, Amazon's search engine and the Internet, it would have been very difficult for people to spread the word about your book. Now, it's easy.

5) Book advances.

Book advances are nice. But they're *advances*, not signing bonuses. You won't have to pay the money back, but if you don't surpass that payment in royalties, you'll earn zero additional dollars.

Advances allow you to support yourself while you write. But you have to assume your advance is the full amount you'll make for your book, because otherwise, you're taking an unknown risk.

You might get an advance, spend a year or two writing a book, and make zero extra dollars after publication.

It depends on your financial situation, but you can either write on the side while you make money elsewhere (thus avoiding risk of ruin), or you can use Kickstarter, Patreon or another crowdfunding platform to get money beforehand.

Most new authors will be lucky to get even a moderate advance.

***

Publishers have nothing but their reputations.

There still is a stigma around self-published books. It's bullshit, but it exists for now. The stigma exists in all industries. YouTube stars make millions, but are considered socially inferior to mediocre actors struggling to pay for rice and beans.

The YouTube stars don't give a shit, though, and can laugh all the way to the bank, surrounded by raving fans.

The public lags behind technological progress, but catches up eventually. Talk to teenagers and you'll see the future of media. My teenage students in that small Czech village didn't know anything about TV networks, but they knew dozens of YouTube stars and praised them like gods.

If you self-publish professionally, virtually no one will know you self-published. You can even create your own virtual publishing company for free, so you can have a fancy name and pretend.

***

If you traditionally publish, you'll make about 10% of sales in royalties, not including the ~10% your agent will receive.

If you self-publish, you'll make ~70% of sales in royalties. (That's for Amazon Kindle, if you price it between $2.99 and $9.99. You'll also get around 60% for paperback, though that varies a bit, based on the price you set and the book's format.)

It would make sense to forego a percentage for marketing help. But publishers **do *very little* to market your book,** unless you're already famous. They will ask you to do your own marketing, which, of course, you can do without them.

A traditionally published book will take at least a year to complete, if/when you've passed the long acceptance process. My self-published book was on Amazon two months after I typed my first word. I had full creative control. A publisher would've censored my potty-mouth and changed things I didn't want changed.

Again, publishers are incentivized to act risk-averse. They will spend money on a book only once it has been proven. If you wind up becoming the next JK Rowling, you'll get some mildly effective advertising money, eventually.

But if you're a normal person, hoping for initial traction, publishers won't help you. You'll have to market yourself.

Fortunately, it's easier than you think, as I'll explain later.

The easiest way to "get published" is to "have a platform." An email list, Facebook page, Twitter following, etc.

But if you already have a platform, you don't need a publisher. You already have access to your core group of readers! They will just tell you to sell to those people, which you can do on your own.

Traditional publishing is slower, less profitable, and you have to beg to get a shot.

Publishers used to control production and distribution (via bookstores). Now, Amazon lets you do these things for free.

You can put a digital and paperback book in front of your readers for free, in seconds. It will look the same as a traditionally-published book, if you do it properly. You have access to sell your book to anyone with an Internet connection.

That's almost four billion potential customers you have access to, for free.

What are you waiting for?

6

Everyone Is Dying

"Anything that's not creative, society can replicate and not pay you full value for." - Naval Ravikant, The Tim Ferriss Show

I know: It sounds weird. *You're saying "getting published" is completely unnecessary? But that's how it's always been!* **Decentralization is happening everywhere.**

In the past, if you controlled manufacturing or distribution, you had power. Creators, artists, entrepreneurs — you had to convince the people with the money that you were *worthy*.

Sometimes it was fair, sometimes it wasn't. Nowhere near a meritocracy. Good people got rejected, bad people got approved, and most people were afraid to try. Some succeeded.

In photography, cameras started out expensive. Now, professional photographers can use iPhones. Distribution was controlled by media companies. Now, you can *be a professional photographer* on Flickr, Instagram, wherever.

In business, you needed lots of money from investors to *be an entrepreneur*. Now, Facebook, Twitter, Uber, AirBnB — virtually all recent big successes started with almost no funding.

Video moved from a bajillion cameras and production companies ... to a dude with an iPhone posting on YouTube. You can *be a professional filmmaker* on YouTube.

Middlemen and gatekeepers are going extinct.

You can go right to your readers and get paid what you're worth. Of course, that's it's own problem. Most work is worth jack-shit.

Anyone *can* publish a book, but only good books will make money.

That's freeing, but it's also scary. Writing a good book is hard.

If readers don't like your book, they won't buy it. You won't lose any money, but you'll lose time and pride and you'll make nothing and be stuck at your day job.

When I realized I *could* write a book, I'd figure it'd suck and I'd make five bucks.

But I pictured publishers: A room of rich, old white dudes telling me I couldn't write do it, said fuck "getting published," and started writing anyway.

I didn't think I'd gain much, but I had nothing to lose.

7

Self Publishing Is Easy As Instagram

"Can I get to exquisite without having to feel really vulnerable in the process?' 'No.' 'Well, shit. That's just awesome.' " - Brené Brown, Daring Greatly

"Getting published" by a publisher is almost impossible when you're just starting. But self-publishing your book on Amazon, in paperback and digital formats, is as easy as posting on Instagram.

Book marketer Brent Underwood proved "it takes $3 and 5 minutes" to become a "bestselling author." Literally anyone can do it.

I didn't feel like writing a book so I instead just took a photo of my foot. I called the book "Putting My Foot Down" and included one page with, you guessed it, a photo of my foot.

He had a handful of friends buy the book. Because Amazon's bestseller rankings are updated multiple times a day — they only care about *recent* sales, not overall — and he intentionally chose a small, noncompetitive category ... Underwood's book quickly became a "bestseller." Technically.

Of course, he did this to prove that the word "bestseller" is bullshit." Bestseller doesn't mean *big* seller. Even the New York Times list is heavily tainted and biased and can be cheated.

The word *bestseller* is for boosting your street cred. Use it if you want. Whatever. That's not the important part.

I got excited when I realized how easy it was to self-publish. You press a few buttons.

But then I realized Underwood made like five bucks.

And most "authors" make like five bucks, selling to their parents.

There's no barrier to entry, so most self-published books suck, just like most YouTube videos suck.

The act of *publishing* a book on Amazon, whether it's a picture of your foot, or the *Bible*, is incredibly easy. It takes five minutes to *publish* a book. Just like *publishing* a video or picture.

Zero investment. Zero risk. Unlimited upside.

But you'll probably make five bucks.

At least that's what I thought. Turns out, I had been an idiot again.

(I don't believe in bragging about being a "bestseller," so I won't address the topic directly in this book. Writing a good book helps, but the following article[1] will give you comprehensive advice. Good luck.)

---

[1]   http://bookinabox.com/how-to-get-on-every-best-seller-list/

8

Wait, The Martian Was Self-Published?

"Few of us take the time to consider. It's not that we're 'inconsiderate' in the sense that we're rude or brash or one of the other myriad associations we've tacked on to the word over the years, but we are often 'inconsiderate' in the sense that we act while seeing the world from only one standpoint: our own." - Colin Wright, Considerations

People treat self-published authors like they treat beer-league baseball players.

Oh, you play for fun a couple of times a week?

Implied: You're not a *real* basketball player.

In that case, possibly true. You are not Babe Ruth.

When I tell people I wrote a book, they go, wow, *how did you "get it published?"*

I self-published.

Oh, so it's like an e-book?

No. It's on Amazon, in paperback and, yes, also an "e-book," like every other book.

Oh. How?

Anyone can do it. You click some buttons.

Did anyone buy it?

Yes. A few thousand people.

Did you make any money?

Yes, over $14,000 in 21 months.

They get more confused when I didn't major in English.

The look in their eyes is priceless. They're not trying to be mean, they just don't understand how someone can ignore Hall Monitors.

It's the look of someone's worldview being shaken, the look of someone realizing you don't have to listen to the *shoulds*. The point isn't that I'm special; the point is that **anyone** can ignore the hall monitors and do things they *shouldn't*.

You can resist the cognitive dissonance, because it's uncomfortable, or you can realize the freedom it implies.

They're locked in from the inside. You don't need any strength, or even a key, to open the door. You just have to realize there's a door, that you can open it, and be cool with the uncertainty that awaits.

Yes, some people write shitty "e-books" that only their mothers buy. They are the beer-leaguers.

Even if someone writes a book that sucks, who cares? Amazon has unlimited, digital shelf space. You can ignore the shitty books.

They just sit there, undiscovered, while you try to write good shit. There is no downside to accidentally writing a bad book. You wasted time, but got practice. The next one might be good.

There's this odd idea that self-published means "e-book," which means, *not a real book*. It's nonsense.

Have you seen *The Martian?*

The critically acclaimed Hollywood hit didn't just come from a book; it came from a *self-published book*. Before that, it came from a series of blog posts.

Fifty Shades of Grey followed the same path.

Laugh all you'd like, but it has sold hundreds of *millions* of books. EL James is the best-selling author on Amazon.com, ever.

Joke's on us for not writing BDSM novels.

The word "self-published book" doesn't mean anything in and of itself. *The Martian* is one. *Fifty Shades of Grey* is one. So is some shitty, scammy e-book about "how to make money from your couch." (Wait, I'm not referring to this one!)

Every book created — good, bad, traditionally published and not — is released as an e-book (called a Kindle edition). You don't need a Kindle to read one. Just download the Kindle app, on your phone, tablet, Kindle, other e-reader, or computer.

As I've explained, you can and should release your self-published book as a paperback edition. It's free. You can even release an audiobook, which I often recommend, down the road.

In general, traditionally published books look *professional.* Self-published books only look professional if you make them look professional.

That requires: a great cover; great, tightly-edited content; blurbs; reviews (social proof). A self-published book can have all of those things, if you know what you're doing. There are good self-published books, and bad. There are good traditionally published books, and bad.

If you self-publish *professionally* — with quality freelance editing and design — your book will be indistinguishable from a traditionally-published one.

My first book has made me $10,376.13 in *profits.* A traditionally published book would have needed to sell around 100,000 copies to reach that number. My book never would have sold 100,000 books. And no publisher would have accepted me, anyway.

The only difference between a self-published book and a traditionally published book is that a bunch of pretentious people loaned you money. Why does that matter?

Dismissing a self-published book that readers like would be like dismissing a startup that didn't need venture capital.

Since there is zero barrier to entry, the floor of a self-published book is low. But just because some people write "shitty e-books" doesn't mean you should.

The floor is rock bottom, but Mars is the limit. And no one will edit out your corny jokes, or swears, biznatches.

Shit, publishers didn't exist when *The Bible* was first written. It was handwritten. Self-published, more or less.

Self-publishing is easier, smarter and more profitable than traditional publishing.

That said, you're probably not going to write the next *Martian*, or even *Fifty Shades of Grey*. The handful of self-published books that make it big are outliers.

If you're like me, you want to write a nonfiction book about something you care about, and you'll be lucky if a couple thousand people like it. Or you want to write a niche fiction book.

Fortunately, *that's* the best way to make money self-publishing. Not by writing BDSM.

9

Writers Can Get Rich (Indirectly)

"Either write something worth reading or do something worth writing." - Benjamin Franklin

S ports journalism took my writerly virginity, so I fell in love with it. I wanted to write for *ESPN Magazine*. The editor-in-chief came to my college to speak, so I stalked him for advice afterwards.

Jobs went to elite, veteran writers, he said. Shit! But there was an exception. A young, hardworking kid named Brandon Sneed.

He had applied the traditional way, and gotten rejected. Like how you and I wouldn't "get published."

Then, if I remember the story correctly (I couldn't reach Sneed for comment), he wanted to write a book, but no publisher would accept a random proposal from a random kid (as I've explained). So he went out, did research and followed a college basketball team around, and wrote the book anyway. (Though it looks like *The Edge of Legend* was eventually picked up by a small independent publisher, which I wouldn't have recommended.)

The book doesn't seem to have sold much, but its value was *indirect*. Sneed's traditional resume-plus-article-portfolio application to *ESPN Mag* put him in a crowded sea of similar faces, many with more impressive credentials.

When you follow the same path as everyone else, you're just a number.

But what's the *point* of sending a portfolio and resume?

To prove to *ESPN* he could write quality, long-form sports journalism. That, plus work ethic, was all editors cared about.

Portfolio + resume was the *typical* way to demonstrate that ... but it wasn't the *only* way.

A book not only made him stand out, but it was actually more effective.

By showing he'd write a book without any promise for money, and writing it well, he proved he was perfect for the job.

He was in a category of one, so he couldn't help but stand out. He received an assignment, delivered, did more, and was off to the races.

Even if the book didn't make a single dollar, it opened the door for a career. Whether you want to be a journalist, author, entrepreneur, speaker, or anything else, your book can be definitive proof of your capability. It builds trust.

Resumes are *signals* of your capability. A good book is *proof* of your capability. Of course, you need to have that capability in order to write a good book. A book is a transparent magnifying glass aimed at your core. You're naked.

That's infinitely more powerful. So if you're calculating ROI (return on investment), make sure to include that variable of *infinity*.

The indirect value of a book is massive.

A book with your name on it is an asset you invested in.

Books are evergreen, isolated experiences. There are a lot of books on Amazon, yes, but when compared to the amount of blogs, they pale in comparison. Blogs get lost in the sea of noise. Books stand out.

They make people ask: you wrote a *book*?

It takes more effort to stand out with a book, but bookshelves are *far* less crowded than the blogosphere.

For a writing career: A book is a portfolio, and advertisement for future work, on steroids.

For a speaking or consulting career: A book is a pitch on steroids.

For getting a freelance or normal job: A book is a resume on steroids.

For launching an online course or new business: A book is a sales pitch and initial marketing on steroids.

For an existing business: A book is a business card on steroids.

Your customer will get to know you, your brand and your product or service, in depth. If you have something great to offer, it'll be obvious to the people who need it, and you won't have to sell to them. They'll come to you.

A book is the ultimate platform builder, and platforms are what writing, speaking, and entrepreneurial careers are built upon.

Even in social settings: Tell people you're an *author*, and they'll raise their eyebrows, impressed. Tell them you're a *writer*, and they'll say that's cute, so is my nephew; he works at the supermarket. (Not that there's anything wrong with that.)

Whenever you're trying to be *picked* for something, over other people: whether applying for a job, recruiting business customers, or getting a date — you'll blend with the crowd if you use traditional channels. Everyone applies to mass job postings, everyone advertises on Facebook, everyone is on Tinder. Those things are fine. They can work. But it's hard to stand out.

In a mass job posting ... Harvard 3.9 GPA looks *just a bit better* than Yale 3.87. Maybe Wisconsin 3.4 is actually more capable ... but in that clusterfuck of numbers ... he sure as hell isn't getting picked.

In crowded channels, people are reduced to numbers and *credentials*. Things like college name, GPA, specific experience matter, because they're the only way to tell people apart.

Everyone knows these details are bad predictors of capability ... but they're better than nothing.

If you're a number in a crowd, but I'm a number in a crowd with a slightly higher GPA, I look slightly better.

But if I extract myself from the crowd and show my true worth, I can stand out.

Spend your energy on the big things that can make you stand out.

Books are the new business cards.

The currency of the Internet is trust.

A good book is worth a thousand blog posts.

A good book is a trust machine.

The story of writers "not being able to make a living" is a myth. You probably won't make a living on one book, but you can build an online course, community, speaking career, product, consultancy, coaching business or service off of one. You just have to be creative, which, fortunately, is what writers are.

My book led to my writing and editing jobs, freelance opportunities, and the business I've launched[2] off of this book.

A book makes you stand out. Studies show that most people *haven't* written a book. Be one of those people, and shitty little signals like GPA won't matter.

---

[2]   www.plat.pub

10

But, But, But!

"Argue for your limitations, and sure enough they're yours." - *Richard Bach, Illusions*

You decided to write a book. But you're not an expert. You also don't have enough to say. You don't know where to start. You're not a good writer. You have no time. You don't have enough money. You don't know if anyone will read it. You don't want to do marketing.

And more.

You're right. You should probably give up.

Just kidding. I had these fears too. They're normal. And they're all bullshit.

If you want to write a book, all you have to do is start writing. It's that simple, even though it's hard.

You might not believe me, but that means you haven't tried yet. Let's nip our buts.

11

But Buts Lie

"You must understand fear so you can manipulate it. Fear is like fire. You can make it work for you: it can warm you in the winter, cook your food when you're hungry, give you light when you are in the dark, and produce energy. Let it go out of control and it can hurt you, even kill you ... Fear is a friend of exceptional people." - Cus D'Amato, Mike Tyson's Trainer

Y ou probably have more fears. I did too. They're all bullshit.

"But I'm not a good enough writer."

"Nobody tells this to people who are beginners, I wish someone had told me. All of us who do creative work, we get into it because we have good taste. But there is this gap. For the first couple years you make stuff, it's just not that good. It's trying to be good, it has potential, but it's not. But your taste, the thing that got you into the game, is still killer. And your taste is why your work

disappoints you. A lot of people never get past this phase, they quit. Most people I know who do interesting, creative work went through years of this. We know our work doesn't have this special thing that we want it to have. We all go through this. And if you are just starting out or you are still in this phase, you gotta know it's normal and the most important thing you can do is do a lot of work. Put yourself on a deadline so that every week you will finish one story. It is only by going through a volume of work that you will close that gap, and your work will be as good as your ambitions. And I took longer to figure out how to do this than anyone I've ever met. It's gonna take a while. It's normal to take a while. You've just gotta fight your way through." - Ira Glass

Writing is a practice. Good writing is an arrow, a trajectory, an intent. Start now.

You'll get good if you care. Write and read your work aloud. Read. Write more. If you don't want to get good, you won't. But if you want to, you will.

You don't have to be a "good writer" to get your point across, especially in nonfiction. You need to be clear. The best writing is the clearest. The most like speech. Most of what people think is "good writing," big words, verbose descriptions—induces yawns and opening Netflix.

All that matters is if your story or information resonates with the reader. They'll tolerate imperfect writing for a good story or useful knowledge. Try.

Read Hemingway, Bukowski, Denis Johnson, blogs, text messages. Follow your curiosity and just *read.*

And if you *really* don't think you can write, read the *Book in a Box Method* and dictate your book.

"But I don't have enough time."

I wrote *Smarts Sports Betting* in 10 days. It's short, I didn't have a job, and I was following an outline I had created, but still. 118 pages is short, but was the right amount for what I had to offer.

This book took a year. But I did it while traveling the world and working almost full-time.

If you have a full-time job, find an hour in your day somewhere. Get up an hour earlier. Write at lunch. Go to sleep an hour later. Write on your public transportation commute, like David Levien. Stop fucking your significant other. (Kidding.)

A very reasonable average writing speed would be 500 words per hour. Closer to 2,000 if you "word-vomit" as I'll later suggest.

That's 15-60 hours of writing, to create a short book. (Though it'll need editing afterwards.) That's 1-2 months of *just one hour a day*. You have time to write a book if it's important enough to prioritize.

"But I don't have enough money."

It's free to publish on Amazon. I spent $5 on a surprisingly sexy cover and edited the book myself. As I'll explain later, I don't always recommend doing things that cheaply. But you *can*, if you were poor like me.

You can also use Kickstarter, Patreon, or another crowdfunding platform to pay for editing and design costs.

As I'll explain later, you can release the book for $5 like I did (or $0), then use the profits to re-launch an improved edition with quality design and editing, later.

Even the highest-quality book possible (which may be smart if you can afford it), will only cost a few thousand bucks.

"But will anyone read it?"

I'll later explain how we will test your idea to ensure it has some traction. You won't write a book until you know people are interested. That's a waste of time.

"But I hate marketing."

I'll later explain that *writing is marketing*. I did no "marketing" for my book. You attract readers as you write, and make your book so amazing those readers can't help but spread the word and market your book for you.

You just write a good book, prepare it properly, put it in front of the right people, and watch them spread the word.

"But I don't have an idea."

You might think you're too young, don't have enough skills or knowledge. You might think you have something to say, but it's been said before. You might not think your message is unique.

This is healthy. It means you're not a sociopath who thinks his opinions are gold.

That said, you *do* have something to say. I'll discuss more in the coming chapter, but take a serious accounting of what you have at your disposal.

What have you done in your *life*? Don't just think of official jobs you've held.

What have you gone through? What have you learned? What do you want to learn? What are you struggling with?

By exploring those answers, you have a book. Information is abundant, but wisdom and empathy are scarce. If you can tell a vulnerable story that helps affects someone emotionally, they'll want to read your book, and thank you for writing it.

Your life experience is your idea bank. That shit you've been through. That shit you've accomplished. That shit you still struggle with.

12

But I Don't Have Enough to Say

"Find things that are 'just not done' in your industry, and then go ahead and do them. For example, JetBlue Airways almost instituted a dress code — for its passengers! The company is still playing with the idea of giving a free airline ticket to the best-dressed person on the plane. A plastic surgeon could offer gift certificates. A book publisher could put a book on sale for a certain period of time. Stew Leonard's took the strawberries out of the little green plastic cages and let the customers pick their own. Sales doubled." - Seth Godin, Purple Cow

"But I don't have enough to say."

A book is just a container for words. Of any size.

How many nonfiction books have you enjoyed, but wished were half as long? Most. Publishers force authors to write books long enough to look good and stand out on a bookstore shelf.

On Amazon's shelves, long and short books look the same. What separates them is what *should* separate them—title, reviews, description—signals of *quality*.

Size no longer matters.

You can write a killer book that's 150, or even 75 or 50 pages.

Some people may scoff, but why? If you're just padding the rest with fluff, *that's scoff-worthy.* 50 pages of value is better than 300 pages of fluff.

My first book was a sparse 118 pages – 20,000 words. Not a single person has complained.

People may read fiction and think ... *I want more* ... but when have you ever thought that for nonfiction?

Your book has no real value if nobody reads it. Respect the reader. Make your book as long as it needs to be, no longer. They'll thank you later.

You're not forcing them to buy it. Tell them what they'll get and deliver on that measured promise.

This is the future of books.

"Books" are a broad category. These words you're reading are a book, like them or not, so is *Fifty Shades of Grey,* so is *The Holy Bible.*

It's useless to compare books to other books. They're just containers for a singular reader experience. Documentaries are videos, as are Tarantino films, as are cat videos on YouTube. We can use distinctions like *film* and *literature,* if we must analyze, but who cares?

"Self-published" doesn't tell you anything about the quality of the content.

Nor does "traditionally published." A lot of traditionally published books suck, too.

Grouping all self-published books together is like grouping all YouTube videos together.

On YouTube, there is plenty of trash no one wants to watch.

There are also incredible films, long and short.

There are also hilarious cat videos.

All of it's different. Some of it's good. Some of it's shit. Some of it is low-brow, but great.

A book is just a container of stuff that holds value for readers.

A notebook is a book. A cookbook. A phonebook. A book with a picture of your face, you sexy beast. A book of *Kim-Jong Il Looking At Things*.

Don't be pretentious. You can write a book that isn't *War and Peace*. As long as you aren't claiming to be *War and Peace*, you don't have to compete with *War and Peace*.

I wrote a book titled *Mein Trump: Hitler and Donald Hump, Travel Time and Fall In Love (Over Micropenises)*.

It's gross smut.

But as long as I tell you that upfront, what's the harm in giving you the option of buying it?

You also have the option of calling me a disgusting weirdo. You are probably correct.

I repeat: A book is just a container of stuff that holds value for readers.

Which words (or pictures, or whatever) of yours hold the most value—words of teaching, entertainment, exploration, silliness?

Like anyone can start a blog, anyone can write a book. Good ones will succeed and bad ones won't. The only difference is that books give you more credibility, and people can pay for them if they're worth the price.

Make your container, you sexy author, you.

Say Less, Make More, Break it Down

You can make money directly on a book, too. As I've obnoxiously repeated, I've made $10,376.13 on my first book alone.

But that can't even cover my first-world, pretentious habits of wanting food and shelter.

One book is almost certainly not going to make you a full-time income. The *Fifty Shades of Greys* are outliers.

Expecting to make a living on one book is like expecting to make the NBA.

But unlike playing basketball, there is a way to make a living directly from writing books.

I call it **The Portfolio Approach**.

The ultimate example is Steve Scott, who has consistently made $40,000+ per month with his portfolio of 22 self-published books.

A more fathomable example is 16-year old Mark Messick, who makes $4,000 per month. Plenty of others have built similar portfolios.

Tons of fiction writers make a living through bundles of books, especially series, aided by cliffhangers. (See *Write, Publish, Repeat*.)

Each book links to the author's email list and other books.

They all feed into each other. If someone likes one of your books, they'll probably want the others. That's the marketing.

If someone likes one of your books, they'll likely want others.

But even if your stuff is great, you could need five, ten, or more books in your portfolio to earn a full-time living. Don't count on it. Treat it as a long-term investment, worth trying if being a full-time author is your goal.

You're building a portfolio of correlated assets. Every asset you add multiplies the value of your portfolio. Compound interest.

For nonfiction books, the Portfolio Strategy is simple.

Take a big topic (say: writing a book, starting a business, getting in shape), and break it down into sub-topics.

Steve Scott has a bunch of books on *writing* (big topic). They are:

- *My Blog Traffic Sucks! 8 Simple Steps to Get 100,000 Blog Visitors without Working 8 Days a Week*

- *61 Ways to Sell More Nonfiction Kindle Books*

- *Is $.99 the New Free? The Truth About Launching and Pricing Your*

Kindle Books

- How to Discover Best-Selling Nonfiction eBook Ideas - The Bulletproof Strategy

- How to Write a Nonfiction eBook in 21 Days - That Readers LOVE!

- How to Write Great Blog Posts that Engage Readers (Better Blog Booklets Book 1)

- Email Marketing Blueprint - The Ultimate Guide to Building an Email List Asset

- How to Find a Profitable Blog Topic Idea (Better Blog Booklets)

- How to Start a Successful Blog in One Hour (Better Blog Booklets)

Some are around 50 pages. But they only cost $0.99. The longer ones generally cost $2.99, because they're still short.

He calls the ~50 page ones "booklets."

I used to roll my eyes when I saw a 50-page book. But I read a couple of his, and was impressed with the actionable advice.

He has a bunch of books on habits, too.

I didn't link to any of those in the Kindle edition because I don't want you to think I'm trying to sell you his books. I've only read a couple.

The point is: **As long as you're upfront about what's in your book, and price it fairly, you can put anything inside.**

People just don't like being deceived. Don't promise something you can't deliver. Scott isn't trying to pretend he wrote Pulitzer material. He wrote short, actionable stuff for specific people looking for a quick, specific solution to a problem. He uses research, personal experience and curation give you tightly packaged, step-by-step, actionable, concise advice.

At first I didn't get it. It seemed scammy.

But aren't his books *more* valuable than hundreds of pages of theory and research that just shows the author spent a lot of time on it? Isn't that self-indulgent posturing?

Wasn't I just jealous he was making money writing, while I was making excuses, but no money, calling myself a "writer?"

For $2.99, you don't have to waste time Googling and poring through good and bad and getting distracted by different voices. It's not my personal style, and you should find your own, but it's a wonderful strategy.

If people didn't like it, then why do all of his books have good reviews, and so many sales? And if people didn't like it, they would ignore the books. No harm, no foul ... just no success.

There are no longer rules for *what a book is*. Write whatever people want. Write whatever *you* want. Short, long, academic, funny, picture-heavy. Be *you*.

Isn't that more respectful to readers, who may only want some of the information? By focusing on one specific topic, it's easier for readers to take action. Then link to your other books, and they can move on if they want.

This is the future, especially for topics where people are looking for actionable advice. Self-help, weight loss, etc.

Find a sector, break down its most common problems, and write an actionable book on how to potentially solve each. Tell stories, be vulnerable and honest.

Hordes of successful books have consisted of curated, connected, re-purposed, edited blog posts. Hordes of successful books have expanded on articles, or even Tweets. **A book is anything between two covers that people might want to pay for.** It could even be free. Put your words in a book if they deserve containment into a single experience for the reader.

The main magic is still in a book's *indirect* value, but the bundle approach is worth looking into.

I probably should have used this strategy for this book, but I'm stubborn and dumb.

13

But I'm Not An "Expert" (Dry Heave)

"Bukowski was a loser. He knew it. And his success stemmed not from some determination to be a winner, but from the fact that he knew he was a loser, accepted it, and then wrote honestly about it. He never tried to be anything other than he was." - Mark Manson, The Subtle Art of Not Giving a F*ck

One of my weekly sports betting features was a competition between me, two notable football "experts," and a cat on a Roomba vacuum cleaner.

I had watched ESPN and their competitors release "expert predictions" every week for years, despite no evidence of expertise.

Every week, my colleague put his cat on a Roomba vacuum cleaner, and placed paper logos for each matchup on his floor. Whichever team the Roomba gravitated to was Roomba Cat's selection.

We based the results on a hypothetical $100 bet for each pick. Roomba Cat sucked: 107-127 (.457), losing $3,2707, placing fifth of seven.

But the two "experts" sucked more. One lost $3,460, and the other,

$5,350. I had nicknamed myself Matt "Not an Expert" Rudnitsky, and yet I came in first, the only one of seven to make (hypothetical) money. Our random reader came in second.

The point wasn't to prove I was an expert. It was to prove that *credentials don't mean anything if you can't back them up*, and in the case of sports "experts," and most "experts," they can't.

My rule of thumb is: If someone calls himself an expert, he's probably not an expert, and he's probably trying to sell you something you don't want. Most experts have no skin in the game, and no accountability. "Expert" is a fancy label with nothing beneath the veneer.

When I quit my teaching job, I needed to do *something*, but when I considered writing a book on sports betting, everyone kept asking: How will you prove you're an "expert?"

The word "expert" makes me dry-heave.

I wasn't an expert, and I refused to claim I was. But I *did* have important things to teach a certain population of people.

How could I write a book without being one of those assholes who claims he knows everything?

I had a crazy thought: What if I was completely upfront about who I could help, what I knew, how I learned it, how I've failed, and what I learned from it all? And more importantly: **What if I was upfront about what I *didn't* know?**

I had gone from diehard sports fan and clueless sports bettor to "good enough to make it a cheap hobby." I had stumbled into turning $100 into $10,000, then lost it all, but learned a lot, and made money after.

There were tons of better bettors out there. Who was *I* to write a book?

How can you write a book on a topic in which you're not an expert?

I had no idea, and I was afraid. But I had to do something, and I had nothing to lose, so I wrote the book anyway.

14

But Is It Worth Your Time?

"All courses of action are risky, so prudence is not in avoiding danger (it's impossible), but calculating risk and acting decisively. Make mistakes of ambition and not mistakes of sloth. Develop the strength to do bold things, not the strength to suffer." – Niccolo Machiavelli, *The Prince*

Yes, I wrote a book in 10 days, revised it, pushed a few buttons and have made over $14,000. It was that simple. Anyone *can* do it.

But it was the result of five years of immersion in the topic (turning $100 into $10,000 sports betting, losing it all, reading countless books, writing hundreds of articles, having countless conversations, and starting a podcast). I had written an outline, and the book was *bursting* out of me, like the time I went on one of those upside-down theme-park rides after an open-bar night. (I puked a lot of beer.)

I'm not trying to scare you. You *can* do it, and you won't vomit. It's *simple*. But not easy.

You have nothing to lose but your time, but your time is valuable.

Should you write a book?

The rest of this book will be encouraging and instructional. But only read on if you know exactly *why* you want to write a book, and exactly *what* you're hoping to get.

If your goals are undefined or unrealistic, you'll struggle to finish, and if you do, you'll fail, relative to your expectations.

It's great to shoot for the stars. But if you're expecting to get rich on book sales alone, your chances are small.

Only write a book if you're shooting for one of these three goals.

1) Building a platform to start/grow/advance your:

a) business

b) writing career (by using it as a freelance writing portfolio, or by writing more books and marketing them within each other)

c) speaking career

d) career-career

2) Making a small amount of passive income.

If you're expecting to make more than a hundred bucks or so per month on your book, there's a good chance you'll be disappointed.

Writing a book is not a sure thing.

A lot of people ask me things like: "How much will I make per hour writing?" The time you'll spend writing could be anything from a hundred to thousands of hours, and there's no guarantee you'll make a good hourly rate.

You probably won't.

If you're asking that question, you're thinking short-term.

Writing a book is a low-risk, high reward, uncertain investment that pays off indirectly, long term.

You need realistic expectations, or you'll be miserable, because writing a book is hard.

If you're OK with this experimental investment, keep reading.

If you're expecting to get rich directly, shut this book and keep your day job. Sorry.

3) Becoming a better writer.

If you write a book, you'll get better at writing books. If your book sucks, there's no downside, except your lost time, which was practice. Practicing in public makes perfect faster than practicing in private. You'll get valuable feedback and fight perfectionism and fear of putting your work out there.

4) Because you want to.

If you aren't expecting to make lots of money *or* use your book as an investment, you can write a book, because you want to. As long as you aren't expecting anything.

I wrote a gross satirical book (that I'll describe in Ch. 12), because I wanted to scratch my own itch, and show people you can write a book for no other reason than shits and giggles.

The only wrong reason to write a book is to make lots of money. Make sure that's not yours, because you will fail.

Most importantly: **Know *exactly* why you want to write a book, and know you'd be OK with the worst-case scenario.**

Is it worth your time if you make no money?

I want you to write it down at the top of your outline that will become your book. Don't forget this. It will keep you going, because things will get hard. But you've nailed the hardest part, that 99% of people skip. You can do this.

What are you hoping to get directly from the book?

Indirectly?

What's the worst-case scenario, and are you OK with it?

Do you still want to write a book?

Write the answers down. Now, let's write a book.

15

But You Have Nothing To Lose

"This could be a self published book. There is no publisher information. Also, page format issues, no page numbers, poor grammar and typos. This is not a book that should be offered by Amazon.

The information is frequently self evident. I would not recommend a purchase at any price." - Dude That Reviewed My Book

I fucked up. I shouldn't have written a book.

Except: My book averages 4.2 stars over 72 reviews, and this is the only review that mentions any of these things. There are page numbers. It *is* a self-published book. I use informal grammar because this isn't English class, and all I want is easy reading for you.

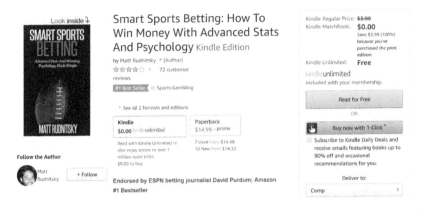

I'm fine with criticism and would happily update the book if a valid concern was raised. (If I can improve this book in any way, please email me *any* criticism at matthewruds@gmail.com).

This person was, objectively, an idiot.

The band-aid was torn off. It hurt for a second. What if the criticisms had been right? I would've apologized, maybe even offered a refund, and updated the book as best I could.

What happens if your book sucks?

A few people will criticize you on the Internet, and forget about you seconds later. Then your book will sit there, unread, criticized.

It's not ideal. But it doesn't mean shit.

Your friends and family, and even most strangers, are rooting for you. I'm rooting for you. People will be impressed and inspired, because the fact that *you* wrote a book means that *they, too,* can do difficult things

The people that matter won't criticize you, and the people that criticize you don't matter.

My final article for SportsGrid was about all of the mean stuff people said to me when I wrote something they didn't like.

First, there was disgraced NBA referee, Tim Donaghy, who called me an "ASSHOLE," and claimed I was friends with some attorney I had never met.

Then, there were the random insults on random articles.

MATT RUDNITSKY IS THE WORST WRITER ON THIS WEBSITE. SO IT'S NO SURPRISE THIS ARTICLE TOTALLY SUCKS BALLS, THIS KID, NOT SO MUCH COMPARED TO MATT'S TERRIBLE WRITING SKILLS.

MATT , FIRST VISIT ROMANIA AND AFTER THAT YOU WILL SEE THE AMERICAN ARE MORE STUPID. SAME LIKE YOU.

MATT IS A JEW FORM URKAINE

MATT,YOU ARE A WASTE OF HUMAN FLESH,,SAD LIFE YOU LIVE!!!!!

MATT RUDNITSKY LIKES PENIS IN HIS POOPER

FUCK YOU MATT RUDNITSKY

EASY TARGET...LOCK AND LOAD WITH YOUR CHEAP JOKES AND SNEERING COMMENTARY...THE DISGUST-ING HUMAN BEING IS MATT RUDNITSKY...

MATT RUDNITSKY CREEPILY USES THE WORD CREEPILY TO AVOID ANALYZING THE MAN'S MESSAGE. WHY DOESN'T HE EXPLAIN HOW BUILDING 7 FELL AT NEARLY FREE-FALL SPEED NEATLY INTO IT'S OWN FOOTPRINT ON 911 DESPITE NEVER HAVING BEEN HIT BY A PLANE? NO MATT, YOU'RE THE CREEP.

MOTHER OF THE WRITER OF THIS STORY HAS A PATHETIC CHILD: AN ACTUAL TRUE STORY ABOUT A WANNA BE JOURNALIST WITH NO TALENT.

P.S. TIM TEBOW IS THE MAN, AND JESUS SAVES!!!!!!!!!!!!!!!!!!

LOL. HE REALLY HAD A SHOT OF NOT FUCKING UP THIS ARTICLE, TOO. AND THEN, BOOM, CLASSIC MATT RUDNITSKY MOVE, INSERTING A FAILED ATTEMPT AT

HUMOR THAT HAS NO BASIS WHATSOEVER. GO BACK TO JOKES 101 BRAH.

YOU CALL YOUR ARTICLE NEWS? WHAT A FUCKING JOKE. MATT, GET SICK.

And all the calls to stop writing.

*DUDE, YOU BLOW AT THIS. PLEASE JUST STOP WRITING FOR THE REST OF YOUR LIFE. REALLY. **JUST DONT EVER WRITE ANYTHING AGAIN.** YOUR LACK OF ABILITY LEGITIMATELY MAKES ME ANGRY.*

*DEAR MATT RUDNITSKY, I HAPPEN TO SEE THIS ARTICLE ON A GOOGLE SEARCH. I'VE NEVER HEARD OF YOU. **I HOPE I NEVER HEAR OF YOU AGAIN.** I BELIEVE YOU ARE THE RACIST FOR INJECTING THE TERM INTO YOUR ARTICLE. YOU ARE AN IDIOT.*

*WHO IS MATT RUDNITSKY?!! OBVIOUSLY A VERY JEALOUS PERSON WHO HAS NOTHING GOOD TO SAY ABOUT ANYONE OR ANYTHING. **PERHAPS HE SHOULD CHANGE CAREERS.***

*CAREFUL MATT RUDNITSKY. **A FOOL SHOULD JUST KEEP THEIR MOUTH SHUT.** THEN NO ONE WOULD KNOW FOR A FACT THAT YOU ARE ONE.*

The best were the calls to not quit my "day job," which these people didn't realize was the job they were criticizing me for doing.

*TERRIBLE ARTICLE. CAN'T EVEN GET THE SEEDS RIGHT, AND CLEARLY KNOW NOTHING ABOUT ANY TEAM BUT YOUR FAVORITE. **DON'T QUIT YOUR DAY JOB.***

GREAT ARTICLE. I THINK YOU HAVE A FUTURE IN

WRITING GREAT ARTICLES. ON SECOND THOUGHT... **DON'T QUIT YOUR DAY JOB.**

YOUR GRAMMAR IS ATROCIOUS. YOU USE PROFAN-ITY. THE CONTENT OF YOUR WRITING IS COMPARA-BLE TO A THIRD-GRADER'S. YOUR BRAIN IS PROBABLY AS SMALL AS YOUR TINY PENIS. LIKE THE PREVIOUS GUY SAID, **"DON'T QUIT YOUR DAY JOB."** *OH WAIT, YOU PROBABLY DON'T HAVE ONE. YOU PROBABLY LIVE IN YOUR MOMMY'S BASEMENT.*

The first few (hundred) insults hurt. Why did people hate the contents of my brain? But I looked at the stats. An average article got, say, 10,000 views. Every six articles or so I'd get one mean comment, on average.

Mean comments are just emotional reactions in the moment. Emotional reactions to ideas, not *you*. A mean comment meant one thing I wrote hit a chord with a reader at a sensitive time. He reacted angrily in the moment and acted, because when you don't see someone's face, it's easy to type whatever comes to mind.

Seeing a person's face makes you stop and consider if you really mean what you're about to say. (Unless you're a sociopath.)

Plenty of non-sociopaths write mean things on the Internet, because there's no face to make them pause.

I'm a very calm person, and yet I've written mean things on the Internet.

Criticism is not worth taking personally.

Once you get insulted a few times, you realize that the .00001% of people who say insult you don't matter. You write for the people who appreciate you, not the people who insult you, most of whom wouldn't hate you if they met you in real life.

And if they would, who cares? They're not your audience.

Your success is measured by the people who like you. The

people who hate you are irrelevant. They just happen to resonate louder in our brains because, through evolution, we've been wired to magnify threats.

But mean words aren't wild animals trying to kill you; they just feel like that. Breathe and laugh.

It cost zero dollars to publish a book.

Mean comments mean nothing.

Even if my book didn't sell, I could link to my book and call myself an *author*. There was considerable upside, and no downside.

I figured no one would give a shit and I'd have to get a "real job," but I had to try. I put my head down and wrote and hoped for the best.

16

The One True But

"Julius Caesar came up from modest means and actually got a pretty late start. When he visited Spain at the age of 32, he saw a statue of Alexander the Great and it put him in a bad mood because he felt that he had accomplished very little (typical GYPSY). And he was just getting started as a priest before a war of rivals in his hometown ended the wrong way and forced him out of that title—so he turned toward the military instead. He rose steadily, both in military rank and political influence, until he eventually overpowered the weak senate, overthrew the Roman Republic, and was declared dictator." - Tim Urban, Wait But Why

There's one excuse that isn't bullshit: Your book might not be good.

If your book isn't good, it won't sell. Most self-published books aren't good, because it's really hard to write a good book. But it's possible. You can't let fear of failure stop you.

Yet I almost let it stop me. When I had thoughts like *I'm not an expert, will anyone care, I don't know where to start, this was a dumb idea, maybe*

I should give up ... those were all my fears that my book would suck, disguised.

The truth is, most people write shitty books even when they have good intentions. And that's OK. You can only intend well and do your best, corny as that sounds.

In *Nobody Wants to Read Your S**t*, Steven Pressfield explains how he stopped writing crap. He's now written multiple successful novels, most notably *The Legend of Bagger Vance*, and multiple successful nonfiction books, most notably *The War of Art*.

I knew I wasn't really writing. Not like real writers wrote. I was sitting in front of a typewriter and pounding out pages, even completing books, but what I was doing had nothing to do with real writing.

What was I doing?

I was using the act of writing (I should say the sham or simulacrum of writing) as a pretense to plant my own ego on the planet so that I could believe I really existed. Have you ever taken a selfie? That was it. That was what I was doing. It was like what people do today on Facebook and Instagram.

I was the hero of the books I was writing. I was the protagonist. I was the point of view. Everything happened to me.

I knew this was bullshit. I knew it was sick, it was sad, it was pathetic. I knew I had to get past it. I had to get over this hump or kill myself.

What was the hump?

One way to define it would be to say it was the watershed between the amateur and the professional. But that doesn't go deep enough.

A real writer (or artist or entrepreneur) has something to

give. She has lived enough and suffered enough and thought deeply enough about her experience to be able to process it into something that is of value to others, even if only as entertainment.

A fake writer (or artist or entrepreneur) is just trying to draw attention to himself. The word 'fake' may be too unkind. Let's say 'young' or 'evolving.'

That was the hump.

To get over it, the candidate must grow up. A change has to happen at the cellular level.

I wrote one novel, and another, and another. Seven years full time, with gaps in between to earn money. And I still couldn't get over this hump.

A couple of years ago I re-read two of these first three manuscripts. I still have them. They're not terrible. But they are excruciating. Scanning a paragraph, I want to put myself up against a wall and slap the hell out of myself, and I would if I didn't have compassion for all of us who are compelled by the nature of life and the structure of the internal universe to go through this ordeal and initiation.

There seems to be no way to make the passage easier, nor any method to eliminate the pain. The lessons can't be taught. The agony cannot be inoculated against.

The process is about pain. The lessons come the hard way.

Most people write selfies. I'm trying not to make this book a selfie, but it might be one anyway.

I recently came across a "story" I wrote in first grade. Reading it, it was obvious I'd become a writer.

My Prized Possession

My Prized Possession is a stuffed animal. It's name is Yankee Bear.
He is gray. He is also soft. I named him Yankee Bear because he
has the Yankee sighn on his shirt and he is a bear. I got him at
Yankee Stadium. My Mom and bought him for me. I got him one
year ago. I sleep with him every night. He is my favorite stuffed
animal.

By,
   Matt

A selfie of the first degree. It offers no interesting information or entertainment to the reader. Booooooo!!!!!

If I were ashamed about a story I wrote in first grade, you'd think I was insane. It was practice. I've gotten exponentially better.

Why should adults treat their work any differently?

I've written articles titled, *Tim Tebow Gets Drunk and Marries a Jew, The 2022 World Cup Will Be Played Inside Of A Vagina (SFW)*, and a book, *Mein Trump: Hitler and Donald Hump, Travel Time And Fall in Love,* under the pseudonym Harry Bearjew (it's OK, I'm Jewish), that included the line, "Speaking of Kim Jong-Un, he'd be totally hot if he has a Hitler stache."

For eternity, that line will be attributed to me. It's awful. Not funny. Who cares?

The Buddha said, "Awake. Be the witness of your thoughts. You are what observes, not what you observe."

You probably didn't expect someone writing a stupid Hitler joke about Kim Jong-Un, spoken by a fictional Donald Trump, to subsequently quote the Buddha. But that's the point. When you write and write and write, you realize *you are not your written words.*

The reason I wrote ridiculous satire about gross time travel fornication is to prove that *you have nothing to lose putting words*

on the Internet. **Unless you attach to those words.**

You change every instant. Your published words don't. Don't attach to them. If you tie your identity to something you've written in the past, while in the meantime you've changed, you're insane.

That would be like holding yourself to things you thought in first grade.

Your words in print are just a snapshot of what thoughts arose at one tiny moment of time in your lengthy life in an infinite universe.

I'll chill with the philosophizing, but this is important in a practical sense.

You wouldn't tie your identity to words you wrote in first grade, so why tie your identity to *any* words you've written? Why let that stop you from growing your career and helping and entertaining people?

They're words you wrote at a time when you believed them. You might still believe in them. You might not. If it turns out they're no longer good, you can admit a change of heart, and even update them. Self-published books can be amended for eternity.

We have a culture of being "right" and not changing our minds, but it's bullshit. Don't be a politician. Be a human who can admit he changed his mind.

I'll write something offensive right now, just to prove my point.

Dogs suck!

Call me horrible. Doesn't matter. Just a snapshot.

It's terrifying when you realize your book might suck. But it's freeing when you realize that it doesn't matter. The act of writing it and reflecting will make you better, and you'll do better next time.

One day you'll be good.

One day I'll be good.

Internally, focus on practicing and getting better. Externally, focus on entertaining people and helping them.

The *Tao Te Ching* says:

> *What does it mean that success is as dangerous as failure?*
>> *Whether you go up the ladder or down it, your position is shaky.*
>> *When you stand with your two feet on the ground, you will*
> *always keep your balance.*

If your intent is to write a good book, but you realize you might fail, you're ahead of 99% of authors. You'll never truly *fail*, and you'll probably succeed externally, too, with patience.

Accept that your book might be a selfie, and then write it anyway.

All that matters is the intent. Are you writing *with* a selfie stick, or did you just accidentally turn the camera around, because writing is fucking hard?

What I'm trying to say is: It's Zen As Fuck to know all you can do is "try your best."

17

Step 1: Treat Your Book Like A Startup

" 'What's new?' is an interesting and broadening eternal question, but one which, if pursued exclusively, results only in an endless parade of trivia and fashion, the silt of tomorrow. I would like, instead, to be concerned with the question 'What is best?' a question which cuts deeply rather than broadly, a question whose answers tend to move the silt downstream." - Robert Pirsig, Zen and the Art of Motorcycle Maintenence

Once you decide to write a book, where the hell do you start? Remember: I was 22, clueless, and only had the courage to start because I was unemployed. I was overwhelmed. So I started with what I knew, what I was already doing. A tiny step.

I wrote my typical, weekly, NFL betting column, but added one thing: Some poorly-written "copy" (I hate that word, but that's what marketers would have called it) asking people for their email addresses.

(ALSO: Interested in learning how to transfer from smart, dedicated fan to rational sports bettor? Email [matt@mattrud.com] with the subject "book" to get free advice on how to start betting on sports, from psychology to money

management to picking winners.)

I collected 46 email addresses in three weeks, wrote articles (potential book chapters) for them, asked for feedback, listened, implemented feedback, and just generally gave a shit about the first people to give me a chance.

I wrote an outline, on which articles had turned into book chapters, banged out the book in less than a month, edited it, got the cover done, pushed some buttons on Amazon, and, boom. My book was available in paperback and digital.

It was out there, on Amazon, like all other books. I went on a celebratory trip with a friend to Dubrovnik and Split (Croatia), and Budapest.

Sitting on the floor in my chairless hostel room in Dubrovnik, I sent an email to my list telling them the book was out, attaching a chapter preview, offering them a 50% discount, and I went out to have fun.

When I returned to Prague, I sent personalized direct messages to about 500 of my ~850 Twitter followers offering a discount. It was tedious, but only took a day.

I haven't done *anything* to market the book since, yet I've made over $14,000.

It seemed so haphazard; lazy even, and I didn't get why it had worked so well. But I've finally realized what I did right. Most people treat books like books. I had treated my book like a startup, accidentally.

18

Step 2: Spy On Your Readers

"It might seem that our job is to build a tribe from scratch, but most of the time, that's not what happens. Nike did not invent the running tribe. There were already runners before runners showed up. Harley Davidson did not invent the outsider tribe — a group that called themselves the 1% long before the other 1% showed up. What we do when we lead a tribe, often, is we find people who are already connected, and we merely show up to lead them. And for most businesses or opportunities, we don't even lead them. We merely service a tribe that already exists. So when you find a group of people who share an instinct, an interest, a connection, a leader, a goal, and you give that group of people something with which they can take action. The way I abbreviate that long sentence is: People like us, do things like this. Once you're able to say: People like us, do things like this; then you have found a tribe that can revolve around what you do." - Seth Godin, The Tim Ferriss Show

T he reason people stress about "building an audience from scratch" is that it's impossible.

JK Rowling didn't create her readers with an Ollivander Wand. She simply appealed to a market of readers that already existed. Then they spread the world.

You find your audience by going where the demand is. It's nearly impossible to create demand as a writer.

Find existing demand, and satisfy it.

That doesn't mean you can't be creative. Find people looking for something general, and give them your unique solution.

Harry Potter readers weren't looking for Harry Potter, but the first readers were people who had previously read *books sorta like Harry Potter.* You can create new art, but you can't create new people.

Derek Thompson explained it best in his *Atlantic* profile of "the father of industrial design, Raymond Loewy."

> *Loewy had an uncanny sense of how to make things fashionable. He believed that consumers are torn between two opposing forces: neophilia, a curiosity about new things; and neophobia, a fear of anything too new. As a result, they gravitate to products that are bold, but instantly comprehensible. Loewy called his grand theory "Most Advanced Yet Acceptable"—maya. He said to sell something surprising, make it familiar; and to sell something familiar, make it surprising.*

Make surprising art. But give it *something* familiar, and start with the people who have already consumed its cousins.

I got my initial readers *from people already visiting a sports blog.*

Ramit Sethi, in his Zero to Launch entrepreneurship class, calls these *fishing holes.* Where do your readers hang out and interact online? (Or offline.)

The answers are endless, but common ones are: Facebook groups, LinkedIn Groups, forums, subreddits, blog comments and YouTube comments.

Anywhere you can listen to what potential readers are talking about, so you can identify their problems, is a fishing hole.

If you have an audience, ask them questions and listen to what they've said in the past. Give them what they're asking for.

If you don't have an audience, study the audience you want to eventually reach.

To find your "niche," ask:

Who are the people I want to affect?

What tribe am I a part of, or who do I want to bring together?

What are problems I've been through and solved, or am going through and want to solve?

What types of things do I read?

Where do I spend a disproportionate amount of my time and income?

Where do these people hang out, in person and online?

Is there anyone in my personal or professional network, even via a friend of a friend, I can talk to for research?

The Internet is like a group therapy session that the whole world showed up to. **People are shouting their problems into subreddits, forums, Facebook groups, Tweets, etc., begging someone to actually *listen.***

They're not talking to you directly, but they're venting in public. Eavesdrop.

Listen, give a shit, engage, and give people what they want. People hate when you try to give or sell them stuff they don't want. But they love when you give them exactly what they want, and they'll usually pay handsomely for it, with a smile on.

A complaint is a demand for a solution to a problem.

Define the problem. Offer a solution. Communicate it clearly, in your audience's language. Use words they use. Empathize.

Research the crap out of your target audience. Interview them. Read reviews of similar books. Pore related subreddits and Facebook groups.

What do they want, that other people haven't given them?

Write that book.

A good idea is: realistic, personal, and *demanded*. You know a lot about it, and you know people want to hear what you have to say.

What sites do they read? Who do they follow on Twitter?

Your audience is already out there. Find them, listen, then engage.

19

Step 3: Steal Readers

"Every individual set of eyes you look into gives you something, whether it's a blank wall or an infinite regress of barbershop mirrors ... (but) bullshit is the glue of our society." - George Carlin, Last Words

You've defined your audience. Now, how do you make them *your* audience?

You're finding them on other people's platforms. You need your own, so you can interact with your audience directly.

Building a website, Twitter, or Facebook page is a potentially worthwhile investment, but **for books, the ultimate platform is an email list.**

When someone gives you permission to email them, that's the most intimate, personalized and visible connection you can have. By collecting your reader's email address, they've given you permission to sell to them. They won't forget about you, as long as you deliver regular value, and continue to keep and build trust.

Collect emails whenever possible.

(Click HERE or email me at rud@plat.pub with the subject "HI" to be included on mine. You'll get weeklyish, free, exclusive tips and stories, book discounts and direct access to me. No spam, unsubscribe any time.)

If you guest post a great piece on a blog, and someone reads it, they'll forget about you in minutes. They have better things to do. But if you put an email signup sheet at the bottom, you've guaranteed that you won't lose interested readers, unless you betray their trust.

Talk to your audience in their *fishing holes*, through guest posts, blogging (on places like Medium.com), Facebook groups, etc.

Tell vulnerable stories. Ask people what they're struggling with. Give away your best tip and ask for feedback. Have individual conversations about people's struggles when they show interest. Record the exact language people use, so you can address it in your book (and business).

Start connecting with these people. Even if it's just your mother, you have *someone*. Help them, write for them, ask them questions, and get them on your email list. *Listen*. Not in a superficial way. These are your true fans. They won't trust you if you don't care.

All you have to do is *give a shit* about your readers. That's surprisingly rare, because most people are so busy worrying about how they *themselves* look. Funnily enough, focusing on others makes you look better.

1) Realize your book starts with an article. It's your minimum viable product (MVP), that validates people want your product/book.

Your articles should be sample/bonus book chapters.

They don't even need to be "articles." This book started with Quora and reddit posts, email exchanges, and Facebook group posts. Offering (hopefully) valuable content for free, not hoarding it, not asking for anything. I was getting feedback. Invaluable.

If they're good and fit in the book, you can reuse them. As long as there's new content, or you're upfront about what you repurpose, you can put blog posts in your book.

Or you can use them as tests that are similar to your book content, then put something different in the book.

Or you can expand on your blog posts for your book.

Or anything else that pops into your crazy head, because it's your book, and nobody can edit out your crazy ideas.

The point is, there are no rules, as long as you're honest and benefiting the reader.

And occasionally you can indulge yourself by writing nonsense, perhaps dropping a self-created word like *pickletits*. Sorry.

2) Watch how your readers interact and engage.

Ask for ideas, feedback, questions, problems. Listen. Engage personally. As Graham writes:

> *Product development is a conversation with the user that doesn't really start till you launch. Before you launch, you're like a police artist before he's shown the first version of his sketch to the witness.*
>
> *It's so important to launch fast that it may be better to think of your initial version not as a product, but as a trick for getting users to start talking to you.*
>
> *I learned to think about the initial stages of a startup as a giant experiment. All products should be considered experiments, and those that have a market show promising results extremely quickly.*
>
> **Once you start talking to users, I guarantee you'll be surprised by what they tell you.**
>
> **When you let customers tell you what they're after, they will often reveal amazing details about what they find valuable as well what they're willing to pay for.**
>
> *The surprise is generally positive as well as negative. They won't like what you've built, but there will be other things they would like that would be trivially easy to implement. It's not till you*

start the conversation by launching the wrong thing that they can express (or perhaps even realize) what they're looking for.

Substitute "product" for "book" and it holds true.

3) If you already have an audience, listen to them!

There are three ways to do this:

a) Ask them.

If you have an email list, Facebook page – any writing audience, simply ask something like:

What would you like to read about?

What's your biggest question about (your vague topic)?

What confuses you about (your vague topic)?

What are you struggling with right now?

If I could wave a magic wand and solve any problem of yours, what would you like help with?

When you write things:

What did you think? Do you have any questions? What else would you want to read?

Listen to the answers. Respond and engage. Are there common threads? That's your initial book idea. Start there, see where it takes you. If it evolves, that's OK.

b) Test ideas on them.

Have an idea? Instead of writing a whole book that nobody will care about ... write a sample chapter or idea as a blog/Facebook post or email. Ask your readers for feedback – do you have any questions? What do you think? Was this helpful? If I could write more about this, what would you want to read?

Listen. Respond. Engage.

c) Hit the archives.

If you've written things in the past — what got the biggest, *most emotional* response? Clicks/hits are not the best measure of *emotional impact.* Comments, emails, shares; those are.

Is there more to be said about that topic? Test it. Emotional responses mean potential demand. Even negative emotions drive sales. Can you believe what this guy said?! For books, all publicity and attention truly is good attention and publicity.

This doesn't mean to troll people; it means polarization is good if it's honest, because of the positive side. People hating you is good, as long as other people love you. You don't want everyone to *like* you; you want some people to *love* you, even if that means some people hate you.

If you've written a book, what did the reviews, emails or Tweets say you were missing?

If other people have written books like the one you want to write, what did those reviews say?

4) Iterate/pivot based on feedback.

More Graham:

> *To benefit from engaging with users you have to be willing to change your idea. We've always encouraged founders to see a startup idea as a hypothesis rather than a blueprint. And yet they're still surprised how well it works to change the idea.*

Substitute "startup" with "book" and it holds true.

Don't let readers control your reading, but consider them and their needs/wants when you write.

(More on this in Ch. 17.)

4) Recruit readers manually, make sure you don't lose them (get them on your email list so you can notify them of your new content).

More Graham: "Do Things That Don't Scale."

One of the most common types of advice we give at Y Combinator is to do things that don't scale. A lot of would-be founders believe that startups either take off or don't. You build something, make it available, and if you've made a better mousetrap, people beat a path to your door as promised. Or they don't, in which case the market must not exist ... Actually startups take off because the founders make them take off.

The most common unscalable thing founders have to do at the start is to recruit users manually. Nearly all startups have to. You can't wait for users to come to you. You have to go out and get them ...

You should take extraordinary measures not just to acquire users, but also to make them happy. For as long as they could (which turned out to be surprisingly long), Wufoo sent each new user a hand-written thank you note. Your first users should feel that signing up with you was one of the best choices they ever made. And you in turn should be racking your brains to think of new ways to delight them.

Substitute "book" for "startup" and it's equally true.

More startup metaphors later, but for now, all you need to know is:

1) Treat articles like test book chapters.

2) Engage with your readers *personally.* Don't expect them to comment on articles unsolicited. Ask your whole audience questions, and also reach out personally to anyone who has shown interest.

3) Treat them like humans, ask them questions, listen, give a shit.

4) Create an email list and link to/embed it in every article.

This is CRUCIAL. People may enjoy your writing, but they're busy and your content will get lost in the sea of crap. If you don't have a direct channel to contact them through, you'll lose readers that *wanted* your stuff.

Do this from the beginning.

Go to MailChimp.com right now, create an email list and signup form, and at the bottom of every article, write something like:

If you liked this, subscribe here for email updates and direct access to me; plus free, exclusive content. No spam, ever.

And then follow through on that promise.

5) Implement feedback, go from article to article to book.

Really, all that matters is: Write good shit that people love, keep getting better, get your readers' email addresses, engage with and listen to them, give them what they want.

You're killing two birds with one stone: Finding and building your audience, while honing your book idea/content.

We like to complicate things with fancy words and tactics. It's simple. But hard.

A short nonfiction book, like most of you will write, is ~25,000 words. That's a lot. But let's say it's 20 chapters; that's 20, 1,250-word articles.

If you write half an article (chapter) a day, 625 words, your book will be done in three months.

If you can write a text, you can write an email.

If you can write an email, you can write an article.

If you can write an article, you can write a chapter.

If you can write a chapter, you can write another chapter.

If you can write 20 chapters, you've written a book.

It's not magic; it's applied consistency to a single focus.

20

Bonus: You're Building Your Publishing Muscle

"Can you make the fear go away? Some people say they can; I'm not sure that it's true. I think that what we can do is dance with the fear ... Once you get into the cycle of shipping, you begin to associate the fear with producing work of value. And then that idea that you can use fear as a compass, that you can say why is this making me nervous — maybe this nervousness is pointing me where I need to go, not the other way around." - Seth Godin, The Tim Ferriss Show

By treating your book like a startup — a series of forum and blog posts that eventually turn into a book — you build your publishing muscle. It's connected to your hip bone. You'll be terrified to put a book into the world, vulnerable to criticism, if you've never done it. If you've been fortified by multiple articles and emails to your list, it will be easier.

You might not notice yourself getting stronger, but, trust me, you are.

I used to be afraid to comment on Facebook posts.

As a blogger, I was forced to publish every day.

Then I quit and stopped publishing and got scared again.

I started blogging again.[3]

Now I write books.

Whenever I stop blogging, the fear returns.

---

[3] https://medium.com/@mattyruds

21

Step 4: Make Your Readers Friends

"Like caterpillars turning into butterflies, prospects go through a five-step cycle: Strangers, Friends, Customers, Loyal Customers, Former Customers. Today, most marketers don't notice, track, or **interact** *with people until they are customers. Some don't even pay close attention until the customer becomes a loyal customer. Unfortunately, a few don't notice their customers until they become disgruntled* former *customers ... they need to have a process in place that nurtures total strangers from the moment they first indicate an interest. At that moment, a suite of marketing messages must begin to be applied.* **The goal is to teach, cajole, and encourage this stranger to become a friend. And once she becomes a friend, to apply enough focused marketing to create a customer."** *- Seth Godin,* Permission Marketing

Are you *really* treating your readers like friends?

Are you *really* giving them free advice and entertainment, asking for feedback, ideas, criticism, listening, and implementing?

If you don't know your readers as *people,* you won't give them what they want.

Humans aren't avatars, even though they appear that way online. Humans are humans, oddly enough.

If you treat the humans like robots, they won't buy your book.

If people aren't paying attention to your writing, you're probably focusing too much on *you.*

You need to build trust, then when you're ready to sell them something, they'll be happy to buy, and you won't feel guilty selling.

If you aren't OK with giving information away, get with the times. You can find any *information,* for free, on the Internet. Hoarding facts is useless.

You have to give away much of your content for free. Basically, you lose money on these "loss leaders," and accept that many of your readers won't pay you directly. But they will pay you in word of mouth, and you'll make up for it by selling premium things, like books, courses, speaking gigs, advertising, products, services, soliciting donations (Patreon, etc.).

As Kevin Kelly explains in *Better Than Free:*

> The internet is a copy machine ... Unlike the mass-produced reproductions of the machine age, these copies are not just cheap, they are free ...
>
> Yet the previous round of wealth in this economy was built on selling precious copies, so the free flow of free copies tends to undermine the established order. If reproductions of our best efforts are free, how can we keep going? To put it simply, how does one make money selling free copies?
>
> I have an answer. The simplest way I can put it is thus:
>
> When copies are super abundant, they become worthless.
>
> When copies are super abundant, stuff which can't be copied

becomes scarce and valuable.

When copies are free, you need to sell things which can not be copied.

Well, what can't be copied?

There are a number of qualities that can't be copied. Consider "trust." Trust cannot be copied. You can't purchase it. Trust must be earned, over time. It cannot be downloaded. Or faked. Or counterfeited (at least for long). If everything else is equal, you'll always prefer to deal with someone you can trust. So trust is an intangible that has increasing value in a copy saturated world.

Trust is the currency of the Internet.

Trust is how you build an audience.

Trust is how you sell books and make money as a writer.

On the Internet, you appear as just another avatar trying to sell people shit they don't want. That's their baseline assumption, because that's how most people act.

So, the best way to build trust is giving people things they want, for free. It pays off, long term.

> *There are a number of other qualities similar to trust that are difficult to copy, and thus become valuable in this network economy. I think the best way to examine them is not from the eye of the producer, manufacturer, or creator, but from the eye of the user. We can start with a simple user question: why would we ever pay for anything that we could get for free? When anyone buys a version of something they could get for free, what are they purchasing?*

As Kelly writes, there are eight "generatives" people will pay for:

Immediacy: Getting what you want, on demand.

Personalization: A version based on your unique preferences.

Interpretation: Support, guidance, explanation. There are hundreds of books on how to play the piano, or do anything, yet people will pay for coaching, or even different, simpler explanations, better metaphors, stories, etc.

Authenticity: Ensuring you get the reliable version you wanted. Like buying a movie from iTunes vs. torrenting.

Accessibility: The ability to use the thing when you want it. Physically, in your possession, or digitally, at your fingertips.

Embodiment: A paperback, a CD, or a live experience. Concert. Yankee game at the Stadium.

Patronage:

> *It is my belief that audiences WANT to pay creators. Fans like to reward artists, musicians, authors and the like with the tokens of their appreciation, because it allows them to connect. But they will only pay if it is very easy to do, a reasonable amount, and they feel certain the money will directly benefit the creators. Radiohead's recent high-profile experiment in letting fans pay them whatever they wished for a free copy is an excellent illustration of the power of patronage. The elusive, intangible connection that flows between appreciative fans and the artist is worth something. In Radiohead's case it was about $5 per download. There are many other examples of the audience paying simply because it feels good.*

Most people won't pay. Doesn't matter. Some will. You just need *enough.*

Findability: Helping people discover what they want. Netflix suggestions, Spotify's algorithm, publishers, record labels, etc.

(Though as I've argued, book publishers do a horrendous job at this.)

Not everyone will be a paying customer. But they will pay you in word of mouth. If they don't, who cares?

Economists like to pretend that you make exactly the value you provide, but that's horseshit. As long as you get enough and help people, shut up.

Louis CK's business model is the ideal aspiration for creators.

You can find his content for free on YouTube. If you watch it and like it, you'll want more, because you *trust* that he's funny.

You can find more content for slightly less than free on Netflix.

When Louis released his new show, *Horace and Pete*, he self-financed the $500,000 tab. News outlets freaked out and claimed he was "millions of dollars in debt!"

Except that he did the self-publishing version of TV, releasing the show online, for $2-5 an episode. People bought it. He's not in debt.

You can watch it for free on illegal streaming sites. People who pay are doing it for **authenticity** and **patronage.**

Not everyone will buy, and that's OK.

He has enough money, because he creates good shit, which instills trust, which makes people buy his good shit.

You may pay a lot for the experience (embodiment) of seeing him live.

You probably won't be as rich as Louis CK, but you can be a poor man's Louis and do quite well.

There are multiple levels of readers and fans.

1) Freeloaders.

People who don't want to or can't afford to buy your stuff. There will be people, even with books, who will scoff at a $2.99 Kindle edition price tag. That's fine. If they consume your stuff illegally, let them. You lose nothing, and may gain word of mouth. You can't change a freeloader with anything beyond building trust and offering them the option to pay.

A freeloader in the book world will refuse to read anything but your blogs/emails. That's fine. They can spend their money however they want.

2) Normal fans

Most people who like your work will buy your cheap products, like a book. Cool. You'll offer them the option for more. Their call.

3) Bigger fans

People who have the money to buy things like experiences — online courses, products, services, etc., and will buy them if the price and value is right.

4) Diehards.

People who will buy everything you produce.

Every good writer/creator has a mix of these fans. Respect each fan for where they're at. Again, treat people like people and you'll build trust and eventually, profits.

Understand each person's demand and capability to pay, give them what they want, and charge them fairly. Don't be afraid to give things away, and don't be afraid to charge big bucks for fairly-priced, highly-valuable things that certain people can afford.

22

Step 5: Realize Your Non-Expertise Is Your Advantage

"There is no smartest person in the room. *Wisdom is the insight that each of us has something to learn from any of us. Great wisdom is the insight that each of us has infinite things to learn from all of us. Living wisdom is the experience that each of us is always learning something new, fresh, vital, life-changing from every single person they meet." - Umair Haque, Three People Not to Be*

I ronically enough, I figured out *why* a non-expert was able to write a successful book about sports betting a few months *after* it became a success.

I'd love to say I'm a genius and figured it out, but I stumbled into it because of that angry Czech mom who made me quit teaching cute rascals.

I had nothing to lose, so I went for it, even though I didn't think it would work.

A few months after publication and success, I was on a coaching call with Charlie Hoehn, entrepreneur and author of *Recession-Proof Graduate,* which details how a college kid with zero experience got to work with Internet celebrities Seth Godin, Tucker Max, Ramit Sethi and Tim Ferriss, and then parlayed it all into a career of entrepreneurship, consulting and speaking.

I was over sportswriting, and I was brainstorming ideas of things to do next, to avoid moving in with my parents and becoming a lifetime bum.

Hoehn said something that stuck with me, even though I've long lost the notebook in which I recorded it.

"Find people you admire and help them get to the next level."

So simple, so profound. Stop and read it a few times. Yes, you know this intuitively, but think about what that means.

Everyone wants to reach the next step in their life.

You want to write your first book.

I want to write my third.

My 62-year-old Dad wants to reach retirement.

LeBron James wants championship number four.

Bill Gates wants to eradicate Malaria.

My five-year old cousin wants to pass Kindergarten and get to first grade.

Everyone has a next step they're reaching for.

That means you can help people who are way ahead of you in life, *if you understand what they want and how you can help them get it.* Successful people have money but not time. Young people don't have money or expertise, but they have time and hunger. It isn't worth it for rich people to spend their time doing anything but their most-important tasks, the things *only they can do.*

I used this idea to get a $5,000 contract to turn a successful, busy entrepreneur's podcast into a book. He would never waste his time transcribing quotes and curating them into themes. I would. He could spend the money without batting an eye, and there was considerable upside in growing his business and gaining new fans.

I didn't tell him I *could* do it. I just went and did it, and showed him some of my work. I emailed him (and his assistant), explained what my work was worth to him (directly and indirectly), and said it would cost zero him zero time and a fair price.

All he had to do was sign off, and he'd receive a product that would make him money and build his audience. How could he say no?

Helping a business get to its next step is how you get a job. Where are they now? Empathize. Then, how can you take the company to the next level, with your skills? And, of course, what's the proof you're not full of shit?

It also works in reverse. Even when I was a 22-year old non-expert, there were *tons* of people below me on the sports betting knowledge totem pole.

I wrote in the introduction:

> *I wrote this book so you don't end up like I did. It sucks to lose $7,896.32, especially when you're a jobless college junior. That's 15,792.64 Natty Light cans.*
>
> *This book gives you every step you must take to leap ahead of the 90% of bettors who don't have a clue. **If you learn all of the simple steps provided you will become ... decent at sports betting.** It will make sports betting a decent investment for you at best, and a cheap hobby at worst.*
>
> *I can't make you a professional, but I can put you on the right path. If you want to make money, you'll first need to know everything in this book. And I'll point you towards the next step at the end.*

Unsurprisingly, I've gotten rave reviews. Not because I wrote *the definitive book on sports betting*, but because I promised something realistic and useful, and delivered. It matters how much you help people, but it also matters how high you raise their expectations. Most people promise the moon by default, even though they can't deliver. Don't.

If I had promised to make people rich, my book would have sucked, even if the content had been the same.

Since most people write books to prove their intelligence, even the few true "experts" often write from a pedestal.

The best way to help someone below you get to the next step is to meet them there, take their hand and help them up. Meet people where they are, and help them up. Connect and uplift, through empathetic storytelling — speaking from *before* the moment of transformation, when things were uncertain — connecting, uplifting.

Most people write books to show how smart they are. For ego. If you genuinely want to help people (which, fortunately, is also how you get people to talk about you, which is how you make money), *you need to transform people.* Make them change. You can't just give them information from a pedestal. You have to connect and bridge the gap.

Speaking from a pedestal is ignorant. You're forgetting the fact that you were once in their shoes, and you're only where you are because of circumstance beyond your control. And your readers are ahead of you in plenty of other aspects in life.

Fake "experts," otherwise known as douchebags, are a step ahead of you, but lie and say they're in the penthouse. They write from a pedestal, make promises they can't keep, and don't help you.

Real experts often write from a pedestal because they've forgotten what it's like to be a beginner. LeBron James wouldn't waste his time writing a book on how to get good at basketball, but if he did, you probably wouldn't relate. *Have good genetics, practice seven hours a day, do cryotherapy, have a personal chef, and get daily massages!* Uh, how do I make my middle school team?

Your inexperience is your gift.

Every time I talk to friends, it's that they don't think a certain goal or transformation is possible *for someone like them.* Your mom may say she can't start a business, because she's too old. *Lean Startup* might give her the nuts and bolts, but it won't help her overcome that limiting belief.

You see people floors above you on the ladder of success, and it's hard to fathom bridging the gap. They can do it, but you can't.

Reading Teddy Roosevelt's biography, I was struck when author Edmund Morris quoted Roosevelt's journal from after his Harvard graduation.

"I have absolutely no idea what I should do when I leave college." - *Teddy Roosevelt*

We forget our heroes are human, because they're invisible while struggling to climb the ladder to that visible pedestal.

Even after reading that striking, unusual sentence, I still felt helpless in the face of Teddy Roosevelt. He had done too much; I couldn't relate.

Reading biographies like that are great for long-term inspiration, but overwhelming when trying to make a short-term change. And relatability like that is rare, unless someone is a lifelong journal-keeper like Teddy.

By meeting someone *where they are now*, you can connect, show them that everyone was at that step at some point, and help them up.

Your non-expertise is your advantage, as long as you acknowledge it.

If you *really* don't think you're an expert, ask: What are you currently struggling with?

By documenting your process and hopefully overcoming it yourself, you'll relate to everyone in your shoes. Like Jia Jang, who failed miserably in his dream of raising money for a startup — so he wrote a book on how to overcome rejection, by intentionally getting rejected every day for 100 days.

It's valuable because it's real.

People's bullshit detectors are sharp. If you try to dress up your flaws, people will know. But if you explicitly acknowledge your flaws, and use them to your advantage, you're not bullshitting. You're being honest and helping, and that's what people respond to.

Still think you don't have anything to say? Bullshit. Everyone has problems, and the ROI of a book is simply focusing on solutions to those problems.

Right out of college and can't get your first job, because you were a liberal arts major and the economy sucks? I'm sorry. But focus on the problem. Articulate the problem. Then ask the question: How can a recent liberal arts grad get hired?

Write a book trying to answer your life's central question.

You won't be the only one who can benefit from the exploration.

By acknowledging your problems but turning your focus to potential solutions and *actually going for them*, you have a book.

The lower down on the ladder you are, the more people you'll connect with.

The less you know, the more people like you, and the more books you can sell.

Most people don't acknowledge their flaws, because they think it will make them seem less credible. Bullshit. Hall Monitors flash their badges at you, but then you ask them for help, and they keep flashing the badge and don't acknowledge your questions.

If someone asks you a question you don't know, acknowledge that you don't know, and do your best to find someone who does. That's what Google and books and life is for.

As long as you're upfront and honest about where you're at, and what you can teach, you'll connect with readers better than a true "expert."

Connection and empathy is what transforms people, and transforming people is what generates word of mouth, and word of mouth generates book sales and income.

You don't have to write the definitive book on a subject. You shouldn't try. Find people one step below you, tell your story, and help them up.

Disarm your critics. If you don't know something, explicitly say it. If you're aware of a deficiency and you don't promise anything, you've disarmed your critics. It's like when fat comedians get on stage and make a fat joke. All of a sudden, that heckler going "you're fat!" has no power and looks like the mean moron he is.

If you haven't reached the next step yet, you can interview people who have, and tell their story, or you can self-experiment and try to get to the next step on your own, and then document your story.

This means anyone can write a book on anything. Want to write a book on how to become a standup comic even though you have no experience? Doesn't matter that you've never done it. That's your advantage.

It's called immersive journalism. Document the journey. It's immensely valuable for anyone who wants to do the same, so they can learn from your mistakes and successes.

As long as you have the *cojones* to get vulnerable and laugh at yourself.

As Richard Bach wrote in *Illusions*, "You teach best what you most need to learn."

For a life of growth, ideally, you'll have mentors *below you whom you can help*, people *at your level with whom you can relate*, and people *above you who can inspire you, show you what's possible, and lift you up*. A book is a virtual mentor, the next-best thing.

Write books that can mentor people.

Don't hide your gift because it's a nice gift card, and not a billion dollar check. The only way to fail is keeping your mouth shut and therefore helping no one. But I still doubted myself.

It was *just* a self-published book. It was *just* about sports betting. There wouldn't be enough people who cared, and they wouldn't take it seriously. And whatever you want to write about: You're worried about the same.

Turns out, that's bullshit too.

23

Step 6: Paint Your Idea Purple

"If you want to tell people the truth, you'd better make them laugh or they'll kill you."—Bernard Shaw

I n *Purple Cow*, Seth Godin explains how to stand out in today's overcrowded marketplace. He tells the story of his family driving through France, "enchanted by the hundreds of storybook cows grazing in lovely pastures right next to the road ... then, within a few minutes, we started ignoring the cows. The new cows were just like the old cows, and what was once amazing was now common. Worse than common: It was boring."

He would have noticed a *purple* cow, though.

The other cows were fine. But they blended together.

As he writes, "**if your offering isn't remarkable, then it's invisible** — no matter how much you spend on well-crafted advertising."Is your book a Purple Cow, or boring, rehashed mediocrity?

Remember: Being good isn't good enough, and being remarkable is better than being good. Even if your remarkable content has flaws.

Like this tyfo.

<h1 style="text-align:center">24</h1>

Step 7: Spell Out Your Thesis

*"The reality is that marketing non-fiction is fundamentally different than marketing fiction. This is because non-fiction is information and that can be marketed under the assumption that **the reader gets an ROI from it, and so your marketing is about showing/telling the reader why this book will help them with some goal they have. Why it matters to them** ... Doesn't work like that with fiction. There is no direct ROI. With non-fiction, you are marketing to anyone who needs your information. With fiction, you are marketing to people who read fiction already. And those people are very difficult to market to. The only consistent marketing I've ever seen work in fiction is writing more (good) books (because that generates the only marketing the consistently works in fiction, word of mouth)." - Tucker Max*

As we've established, nonfiction books are generally intended to help people get to the next step in their life. To solve a problem, or become something.

For narrative nonfiction, you're telling a story people like you want to hear, for entertainment.

So, you're generally writing to one of these avatars:

1) Your past self (how you overcame a past problem).

2) Your current self (tell a story you want to hear).

3) Your future self (investigate a current problem you have, via interviews, case studies, and self-experimentation).

You need to make the book's ROI clear to the reader. You also need to make sure it *has* a significant ROI.

Write it down. Use what prolific copywriter Ray Edwards, in his book *Write Copy That Sells*, calls your *copy thesis*.

"Any [YOUR AUDIENCE] can [SOLVE THEIR PROBLEM] by using (reading) [YOUR PRODUCT], because [HOW IT SOLVES THE PROBLEM]."

If you already have a business, what benefits do you sell?

Benefits are different from features. Features are the information, benefits are how the reader is transformed, and what they get.

Weight-loss recipes for mothers are *features*. What those recipes provide for *busy mothers* — time saved so that they can go to Jimmy's soccer game, and extra energy to play with Jimmy afterward, are *benefits*.

If you don't have a business yet, what has your research told you your customers want?

Go the extra mile. Why do they want what they want? What will it get them? How can you help them achieve that dream?

A book on how to **become** something is very powerful.

This means you need to actually think of your reader *before* writing. Will they give a shit? Who are they, before this transformation? What's the story in their head? Empathize.

This sounds basic, but unless you have an avatar — a picture of your ideal reader and what they'll get from the book — you're just guessing, and humans are horrible guessers of what other humans like.

As Kurt Vonnegut said, "Write for just one reader."

Get super-specific. For me, it wasn't "Any [SPORTS FAN] can [MAKE LOTS OF MONEY] by reading [SMART SPORTS BETTING], because [IT GIVES THEM STEP-BY-STEP ADVICE ON HOW TO PICK WINNERS].

It was: "Any [DIEHARD NFL FAN THAT ALREADY BETS BUT DOESN'T WIN LONG-TERM] can [MAKE SPORTS BETTING A CHEAP, STRESS-FREE HOBBY] by reading [SMART SPORTS BETTING] because [IT GIVES THEM STEP-BY-STEP ADVICE ON HOW TO CHANGE THEIR MINDSET SO THEY DON'T MAKE THE BIG, COMMON MISTAKES].

I intentionally promised less, for a smaller audience. Ironically, it led to more sales. Honing in on a smaller target is more effective than trying to hit a big target, because it's much further away, and everyone is going for it.

Help your readers achieve/become what they want. That's your book. You get customers by helping people and building trust, and you do that by solving their problems. Give them everything they need. Then for people who need the next step, for you to walk them through it, offer them a course, coaching, another book, etc.

A good friend listens to you and helps when you ask them. A great friend shows up with exactly what you were looking for, before you even knew to ask.

Same with writers or entrepreneurs.

How well do you know your audience?

Remember, the way to self-publishing success is:

Find a small group of people that *love* your work. Not a large group of people that *like* your work. Only lovers talk about you and spread your book.

This means you need to connect and resonate emotionally, and **know**

what your audience wants better than they do.

25

Aside: For Fiction, Memoir And Books Without ROI

"Storytelling is all about making the reader ask: What happens next?" - Brian Grazer, A Curious Mind

This book is mainly written for informational nonfiction books, because they're the simplest to market.

Obviously, though, there's a large market for stories that don't have a clear ROI — fiction, memoir, narrative nonfiction, etc.

I've worked with authors on these and am writing my own, and there are a few important principles to understand.

1. People read fiction and narrative nonfiction mainly to be entertained and/or learn something. To do that, you need to *hook them*, and *connect emotionally* through some sort of theme. This is vastly oversimplified; read *The Story Grid* and *Nobody Wants to Read Your S**** for detailed explanation on why that's essential.
2. If you write fiction, you're marketing to people who *already read fiction*. It's virtually impossible to sell a fiction book to a non-

book-reader. Study your audience, whether it's sci-fi or historical fiction or whatever, study your competitors on Amazon, and market to those people.

3. Your best marketing will be writing more books.
4. For fiction, things like series are the best marketing, because they feed into each other.
5. Your biggest challenge will be finding your core audience.

The same principles apply; they're just more difficult. Find blogs and forums and subreddits and whatnot where your genre's readers hang out. Post short stories or sample chapters. Check out places like Wattpad, where you can build a platform in a reader *fishing hole*. Leave cliffhangers. Build your email list.

Use the same exact principles as we've discussed.

1. Find where audience is already hanging out.
2. Give stuff to audience.
3. Get their emails.
4. Write a book, consider splitting it up into series with cliffhangers.
5. Make it good so people talk about you.
6. Write more books and link to each within each, and, of course, your email list.

26

Step 8: Tell People Not To Read Your Book

"The goal is not to do business with everybody who needs what you have. The goal is to do business with people who believe what you believe ... If you talk about what you believe, you'll attract those who believe what you believe ... What you do simply proves what you believe. People will do the things that prove what they believe. The reason that person bought the iPhone in the first six hours, and stood in line for six hours, was because of what they believed about the world and how they wanted everybody to see them. They were first. People don't buy what you do, they buy why you do it ... By the way, (MLK) gave the 'I Have a Dream' speech, not the 'I Have a Plan' speech." - Simon Sinek, Start With Why TED Talk

When my second month's royalty check arrived and said $1,150.06, I spat out my coffee (figuratively), pleasantly shocked.

I had tried to build an email list off my weekly sports betting column, which averaged ~30,000 hits, but I only gathered 46 emails. I released the book to those 46 people, direct messages ~500 Twitter followers, did no other marketing, and two months later, received $1,150.06.

Huh?

It had all been word of mouth.

I realized: **The way to make money online isn't to appeal to the masses a little bit. The way to make money online is to appeal to weirdos like you, *a lot*.**

Quality of readers, *not* quantity.

When people *love* your book, they talk about it. The emails and Tweets I had gotten suggested my few readers didn't like my book; they *loved* it.

Your quirks are your goldmine.

What do you like that you could never find people who relate to?

What's that thing you like that only a few people you know share? Or, worse, what's that thing you can't talk to anyone about, because no one gives a shit? What did you get made fun of for, or keep secret, in high school?

That's your niche.

Maybe there was only one other kid in your high school who liked anime, Extreme Ironing, or collecting naval fluff. When you're confined to a small geographical location, anything non-mainstream feels lonely. On the Internet, all non-mainstream people congregate, so there are thousands of former-loners you can talk to, who like the weirdest things.

Reddit has *hundreds of thousands* of niche communities. Find your like-minded weirdos. Browse subreddits, from stoicism to drug nerds to Canadian graffiti.

On the Internet, there's a niche, and community, for everyone.

Most people's books are going to be for niche versions of typical things. Are you an expert on marketing ... for personal food blogs? Are you an expert on getting a job ... wait, no, your first *writing* job ... wait, no, your first *job writing for a sports blog*? I'm discussing blogs because that was my world. What's your world? What do you do instinctively on Sunday afternoons?

As Tim Ferriss writes in *The Four-Hour Workweek:* Where do you spend a disproportionate amount of your income? Where are you price-insensitive?

The more specific, the better. Specific books didn't have a broad enough appeal in the past to warrant an investment for publication. Now that fixed costs are ~$0, we're in an era of specialization.

Shit, if you could write the *perfect* book for a rich person, maybe you could charge $10,000 and one sale would be enough. Specialization could theoretically go as far as *personalization*.

As explained, your book generally needs an ROI, because people read nonfiction books to learn, get, or become something.

Author and entrepreneur James Altucher says people on the Internet generally pay to "get paid, get laid or lose weight."

That's oversimplified, sure. People pay for other things. But those are indeed the primary ones, and they don't have to be as scammy as they sound.

My sports betting book was technically how to "get paid," and that's how I sold it, but inside, it was a realistic view on the risks involved.

Get paid, get laid, lose weight focuses on *benefits*. Those are three of the biggest benefits people are looking for, and there are millions of potential books to help people get these three things.

You might think the market is saturated, but most books are too broad to help people get what they want. Production hasn't caught up with specialization. We need more niche books. Hence so many unhappy, unwealthy, unlaid people.

Ask:

What does reading your book get the reader?

How will it change them, and make their life better?

What's different about your particular solution?

In copywriting parlance, sell benefits, not features. Tranformation, not information.

Anyone can get information through Google. People need stories, empathy, customization, curation, guidance, etc.

What's that one specific thing *you're* an expert in, and how does *that specific thing* lead to people making more money?

You need to find *your* unique advantage. It's probably something weird. Have you taken an unusual career, educational, or life path?

What have you learned, and who, exactly, can it benefit?

The smaller the audience, the better.

Writing a book on sports in general was too vague, even sports betting in general, but NFL betting for serious fans who bet recreationally? That's more niche, and I knew exactly where they stood, and what they needed to get to the next level. *Because I had been them.*

The reason Hollywood dumbs things down is because their fixed costs are so high, they need to appeal to the most people possible. Quantity, not quality.

Same with publishers.

But when fixed costs are zero, like in self-publishing, your goal is to appeal to a small niche *a lot*. In a perfect world, those people will spread the word to other niches and you'll blow up into stardom, but even if you stay within that initial niche, you should be able to make a living.

Nobody has to pay your fixed costs, so you can appeal to fewer people and still make money.

You just need, as Kevin Kelly explains, 1,000 **True** Fans.

> *A creator, such as an artist, musician, photographer, craftsperson, performer, animator, designer, videomaker, or author – in other words, anyone producing works of art – needs to acquire only 1,000 True Fans to make a living.*

A True Fan is defined as someone who will purchase anything and everything you produce. They will drive 200 miles to see you sing. They will buy the super deluxe re-issued hi-res box set of your stuff even though they have the low-res version. They have a Google Alert set for your name. They bookmark the eBay page where your out-of-print editions show up. They come to your openings. They have you sign their copies. They buy the t-shirt, and the mug, and the hat. They can't wait till you issue your next work. They are true fans.

You have to start this way. Yes, you may want more. But this is the way to start.

This small circle of diehard fans, which can provide you with a living, is surrounded by concentric circles of Lesser Fans. These folks will not purchase everything you do, and may not seek out direct contact, but they will buy much of what you produce. The processes you develop to feed your True Fans will also nurture Lesser Fans. As you acquire new True Fans, you can also add many more Lesser Fans. If you keep going, you may indeed end up with millions of fans and reach a hit. I don't know of any creator who is not interested in having a million fans.

You get fans by finding where they already hang out online, and gaining their *trust* by giving them stuff they want, and treating them like humans.

This explains *The Tim Ferriss Effect,* coined by Michael Ellsberg, who saw his book sales explode after being featured on Tim Ferriss's one-man blog — as opposed to the minimal boost he got from appearing to the masses on national television.

It's better to be exposed to a comparatively smaller group of people who are engaged, devoted and passionate, *than to a much larger group of people who are casual readers.*

To start, it's great to utilize another person's fans to find your own. Or a platform that has an audience, like Facebook groups, forums, subreddits, etc.

That might seem manipulative. It's not.

If all you're doing is offering free help to people who want it, you're not being manipulative. Don't sell anyone anything unless they've proven they want it. Then when you sell, you're doing them a favor. They'll be happy to buy.

By getting to know your audience, you won't bother anyone, and then when you do sell things, you'll have a very high conversion rate, and both sides will be happy.

Seth Godin calls it *Permission Marketing.* It works, and it makes people happy.

The currency of the new economy is trust. In the social media age, everything is transparent.

Big corporations can still profit because they control resources and therefore can take advantage of people, but you can't do that as an independent author or entrepreneur. And corporations' strongholds are crumbling as decentralization spreads.

Build trust or die.

Since production is free, all that matters is: *How much* **do people love and trust you?**

Not *how many people* love and trust you. Rather: *How much.* It can be a small number of people. But it's the intensity of their fandom. Not if you make them grin, but if you make them beam and cry and act and *change.*

You gain trust through honest authenticity. Your quirks are

your moneymakers.

If you don't build trust, you won't generate word of mouth. Word of mouth is the only reliable long-term book marketing (and it drives Amazon SEO).

About 30 people bought my book from my initial "marketing." The rest was all word of mouth and Amazon.

All because I intentionally wrote about something that I *knew* wouldn't have mass appeal. Don't write the book you think the most people would read. Write the book that a small group *can't not* read and recommend. Write the book that only *you* can write.

Don't write about losing weight; write about how 30-something female surfers can lose weight via an all-fish diet in the Upper East Side.

Start with them. If your book is good, they'll tell their 40-something female surfer friends, who will tell their children, and soon after everyone will be thin.

27

Step 9: Outline Non-Anally

"I shudder to think of how much brilliant work was abandoned simply because of a lack of certainty. Moves that appear the least risky in the short term are often the most risky in the long term, because they keep you among the huddled masses of those who are doing expected, mediocre work. The unspoken truth is that very few people ever become comfortable with risk, but brilliant contributors recognize that without measured risk in your life you will not grow." - Todd Henry, Louder than Words

I'm a freelancer for Book in a Box, a company that turns people's ideas into books, when they don't have the time or desire to actually write, but they do have money. They wrote a book on how to use their process on your own if you can't afford to pay them (it's a high-end service).

The book is a fantastic read, especially if you'd rather dictate your book than write it, and their outlining section is too good to not summarize here.

Before you start, hone in your book idea by asking some of the questions they recommend. You know generally what your book is about. But what are the essentials that need to go in the book. Get your ego out of the way. What does the audience want and need to read?

The following are quotes is from the book. Read the whole thing. I don't have any stake in the book; I just love it.

"What is the story my readers told themselves (about the world, about their situations, about their perceptions) before they started my book? How does my book fit into those stories, and what part does it play?"

For me, many people said (and I know this through research and conversations):

- I'll write a book ... *eventually*.
- I want to "get published."
- Self-publishing is ego-stroking and unprofitable.
- Writing a book is hard ... I could never ... or at least not yet.

"What does this mean your book should be about?"

"What is the essential point(s) you are making for your audience? What are the main points you want the audience to take away from your book?"

Mine are:

- You can start writing a book today.
- It is a smart financial and personal decision for many people ... as long as they're realistic.
- Self-publishing is more profitable than traditional publishing, provided it's done right.
- You can do it right by following the 11 steps in this book.
- Writing a book is hard, but doable.

None of those points are about me. Initially, my ego wanted me to write from a pedestal and tell you: Here are my top writing tips! Use the software I use! Use the language I use! Make dick jokes like I do!

No.

Your book is for your reader, not you.

"What background information does the reader need to have to understand your points above? How do you plan to explain all the background information that the reader needs?"

What's the story your readers are telling themselves?

How can you meet them where they are, build a bridge, and take them where they want to go?

That's true empathy.

"The Double-Check Question: How will people describe this book to their friends?"

"What will people *really* say about this book? Not what you *hope* they say."

My plan is: The book shows you how to self-publish profitably and legitimately ... without BS promises.

The Book in a Box Outline Template

Book Information

- Working Title/Subtitle
- The Promise/Value Proposition/Quick Summary
- Anticipated Audience(s), and Their Benefits From Reading

Table of Contents
Introduction: [Working Title]

- What's the hook?

1. What's the pain of not reading the book?
2. What's the pleasure of reading the book?
3. What will the reader learn, and why will that make them happy?

Part 1: [Working Title]

- Description/overview

Ch. 1 [Working Title]

- [Subpoint 1]
- [Story 1]
- [Optional: Support]
- [Subpoint 2]
- [Story 2]
- [Optional: Support]

Conclusion

- Reworded Thesis
- Optional: Story that summarizes book.
- Summary of all the main points.
- Where to learn more/call to action page.

***

The book explains every element fully, but those are the basics. Don't ignore outlining because it's unsexy.

I initially tried to write all three of my books without outlining — I didn't want it to hamper my creativity — and I spent months wandering aimlessly.

Constraints facilitate creativity.

You can always adapt the outline. That's why I said *non-anally*. Outline so you have a loose structure, then see where it takes you. Don't be afraid to change the outline on the fly.

An outline is just a set of guiding posts.

Don't be afraid to venture a bit outside, or move the posts. But they're essential so you have some direction at first. An outline gives you an estimated finish line and checkpoints on the way. An outline gives you peace of mind. You don't have to stick to it.

Writing a book without an outline is too daunting for most people. It set me back months. It sucks and makes you feel stupid. There's no downside to having an outline, unless you refuse to pivot as you work.

Outline, then write one chapter at a time. Treat them like articles.

A 25,000 word book might seem impossible, but what about 25, 1,000-word articles on the subject you know most about?

28

Step 10: More Research!

"The story is told that the great scientist Einstein was once asked how many feet are in a mile. Einstein's reply was "I don't know. Why should I fill my brain with facts I can find in two minutes in any standard reference book?" - David J. Schwartz, The Magic of Thinking Big

Have you read (at least) the best five books in your category? Have you talked to dozens of potential readers? Then how do you know what they want?

I read about a book a week, am constantly highlighting and taking notes. This book synthesizes about a dozen books and blog posts. Never. Stop. Researching.

For a writer, life is a massive batch of book topics to research, investigate, and reflect on. Your curiosity is your compass.

For people writing one book, you don't need to be as anal. But you do need to know your topic inside-and-out. Reading the best few books in your category is essential.

This is more useful "marketing" than buying ads and shoving your book in front of people who don't know you and wouldn't read your stuff even if they did.

Spend more time researching than "marketing."

Spend time to cultivate an audience you *know* wants and needs your stuff. Then "marketing" and selling will be easy.

Never stop getting to know your readers as *people.*

But remember: Even if people say they're looking for facts, they're not. Everyone wants emotion, experience, *affect.*

29

Step 11: Get Scared

"Are you paralyzed with fear? That's a good sign. Fear is good. Like self-doubt, fear is an indicator. Fear tells us what we have to do. Remember our rule of thumb: The more scared we are of a work or calling, the more sure we can be that we have to do it ... If it meant nothing to us, there'd be no Resistance." - Steven Pressfield

Are you afraid of starting? Getting stuck in the middle? Giving up? Not finishing? Never getting it perfect?

Good.

That's a sign you're on the right track.

If you're not a little (or a lot) scared, you're irrationally confident and your book will suck.

And you need to read Steven Pressfield's *The War of Art: Break Through the Blocks And Win Your Inner Creative Battles.*

Being scared is good.

"Have you ever watched Inside the Actors Studio? The

host, James Lipton, invariably asks his guests, "**What factors make you decide to take a particular role?**" **The actor always answers: "Because I'm afraid of it."** The professional tackles the project that will make him stretch. He takes on the assignment that will bear him into uncharted waters, compel him to explore unconscious parts of himself. Is he scared? Hell, yes. He's petrified...

Like a magnetized needle floating on a surface of oil, Resistance will unfailingly point to true North - meaning that calling or action it most wants to stop us from doing.

If you're not scared, you're not writing the right book.

Listen to your fear (the *Resistance*). Laugh at it. Thank it for showing you the way. It's like an ex-girlfriend or boyfriend, or your dick boss, Richard.

You have to accept looking dumb. Own it and laugh at yourself. Because if you never look dumb, you'll never become smart.

There are probably a few (dozen?) times reading this book you rolled your eyes and went, *duh*. Well, I'm trying to look dumb so I can get smarter and help you as much as possible. Sorry.

I'm doing my best, which means I often look like an idiot. Your fear is your compass.

30

Step 12: Chill

"The problem is that bad writers tend to have the self-confidence, while the good ones tend to have self-doubt. So the bad writers tend to go on and on writing crap and giving as many readings as possible to sparse audiences. These sparse audiences consist mostly of other bad writers waiting their turn to go on, to get up there and let it out in the next hour, the next week, the next month, the next sometime. The feeling at these readings is murderous, airless, anti-life. When failures gather together in an attempt at self-congratulation, it only leads to a deeper and more, abiding failure. The crowd is the gathering place of the weakest; true creation is a solitary act." - Charles Bukowski

E very aspiring writer wants to write a book *one day*. I hear it all the time, from smart people age 20 to 60, who like to write. If you don't think you're ready, that means you're ready. Most good writers are perfectionists.

The fact that you're afraid to write means you have good taste and the intention to be good.

That's all that matters. Smile, breathe, and get to work.

Every good writer has doubt while writing.

Stephen King said, writing fiction is like "crossing the Atlantic Ocean in a bathtub ... I'm afraid of failing at whatever story I'm writing – that it won't come up for me, or that I won't be able to finish it."

John McPhee said, "To feel such doubt is a part of the picture – important and inescapable," he says. "When I hear some young writers express that sort of doubt, it serves as a check point. If they don't say something like it they are quite possibly, well, kidding themselves."

George Orwell said, "writing a book is a horrible, exhausting struggle, like a long bout of some painful illness."

Gustave Flaubert said, "I am irritated by my own writing."

If you *don't* get stuck and doubt yourself at all, you're going to fail.

Being scared isn't just normal; it's a requirement of good writing.

It shows you have what it takes. Only people with bad taste are fearless, because they don't know what good work looks like. They write shit, ignorant of the stench.

But you'll only succeed if you sit with the fear, breathing, smiling and writing anyway. As Pressfield writes, "Rationalization is Resistance's right-hand man. Its job is to keep us from feeling the shame we would feel if we truly faced what cowards we are for not doing our work ... **Resistance will tell you anything to keep you from doing your work.**"

I'm not good enough ... no one cares ... this isn't worth my time ... will I make enough money ... will people understand me ... do people want to hear this ... how will I ever finish ... how will I ever start ... this sounds like shit ... I'm hungry ... I'll just go out for a beer ... I suck so bad ... I should go back to where I came from ... I'm just going to sit on the toilet even though I don't have to poop ...

Everybody has these thoughts. They're normal. They're not *you* talking; they're the Resistance. The voice in your head is not you, and it's trying to trick you from doing your best work.

Take a deep breath while the thoughts circle, and write anyway.

The paradox is: good writers are smart. And the smarter you are, the better you are at rationalizing *not writing*.

The smarter you are, the better you'll be at explaining why you can't write.

Remember Pressfield's words: "Resistance is always lying and always full of shit."

31

Step 13: Make Writing A Habit

"It's not the writing part that's hard. What's hard is sitting down to write. What keeps us from sitting down is Resistance." - Steven Pressfield, The War of Art

For the first 18 years of my life, I thought I was a "math and science person," and I never wrote anything that wasn't assigned in school.

Now, I spend hours a day writing, have published three of my own books, and ghostwritten multiple others.

How?

I decided I liked sportswriting and became a sportswriter.

First, I was a journalist with "writer's block."

Then I had deadlines. I met them. It's Parkinson's Law, that "work expands so as to fill the time available for its completion."

Then I became a sports blogger. If I didn't write 6-8 articles a day, I'd get fired. I wrote 6-8 articles a day.

A few years before, I didn't write a single thing for fun, ever. I had no deadline, no clear tasks, no reason to write.

I went from writing zero things per decade to 200+ a year. Now, multiple books.

Pretentious writers tell you things like: "Writing is easy. Just sit in the chair and write."

In a literal sense, sure.

Getting in perfect shape is just eating less and moving more. Going to Mars is just sitting in a spaceship's passenger seat and falling asleep. Solving world hunger is just giving everyone food.

Are you really going to "sit in the chair every day and write" if you have a day job, or kids, or Netflix?

Sitting in the chair regularly, when you have other important and/or fun stuff to do, is very hard.

You "sit in your chair" and do whatever your job is every day. When you're forced to work, you work. But if writing isn't required of you, it's a battle to get in the chair.

As soon as I quit my sportswriting job, I didn't write a word for months, despite considering myself a "writer."

As soon as I stopped being forced to write, I stopped writing. Even though I loved writing.

But then I wrote a 25,000 word book in a week, and have written millions of words since.

I've read dozens of books on willpower, creativity and habits — trying to figure out how to stop *not writing* when I actually want to write — and the solution is simple.

Make writing a habit.

Whether it's a lifelong habit of writing, or a short-term one for your one book, **you'll never write regularly if you don't make it a habit.**

The problem is, every time you do something hard that isn't a habit, it depletes your willpower. It's hard to go to the gym on Monday at 6am. You can do it, but it depletes your limited willpower.

As F.M. Alexander wrote, **"People do not decide their futures.**

They decide their habits, and their habits decide their futures."

You need to use your limited willpower to create the right habits, so you can make doing the right thing the easy thing.

Your brain craves this conservation of energy, making things habitual, and therefore, easy.

Every time you try to sit in the chair, when sitting in the chair isn't forced or a habit, you're fighting a battle. You'll lose all the time, and even if you don't, you'll be weak for the actual writing.

It took me dozens of books to come to this obvious realization, but I'm dumber than you. You can read the books if you're interested in the science — *Willpower, Tiny Habits* and *The Power of Habit* are my favorites — but you only need to know three things.

1. Your brain craves habitual behaviors because they save energy.
2. It takes significant willpower to create a habit, but little to maintain a habit.
3. Your willpower is a limited resource.

Focus all of your willpower on building a writing habit now, so it becomes effortless. Don't do it in conjunction with another habit, whether it's trying to lose weight, gain weight, or wait until marriage to do the sex.

Ideally, you'll write every day, but I refuse to give any hard-line rules. There are always exceptions, but almost everyone *can* write a little bit every day.

I know you probably have a day job. Get up an hour earlier, or cut out an hour of nightly TV. Write on your 30-minute subway commute, or when you typically check Facebook, or on your lunch break. Write whenever. Find at least 15 minutes, or an hour or more if you can, and write every day. Or every weekday.

If you're certain you can bang out a book by marathoning on

weekends, go for it. But you'd better monitor your results and prove you're right. The easiest person to delude is yourself.

Start small. If you're busy, start with 30-60 minutes. A time you *know* you can commit to, long term. 15 minutes if you have to. If you start with a goal too ambitious, you'll fail eventually, and you'll get discouraged.

It's better to hit an unambitious goal every day, than hit an ambitious goal for a week and then quit because it's hard.

If you want to *be a writer*, you'll need a lifelong habit. If this is just for one book, maybe you can be more ambitious, short term. Big goals can work short term, but sticky habits win long term.

Charles Duhigg's *Power of Habit* lays out exactly how to build a habit, scientifically. It's a four-step process.

1. Have a cue (trigger for the habit to start)
2. Define the behavior itself, specifically, and what success is.
3. Give yourself a reward for actually doing the task.

I'll elaborate.

32

Step 14: Find Your Triggers

"(Thomas) Wolfe's prose has been criticized for its overindulgence and adolescent character, so it's interesting to note that the novelist practiced a writing ritual that was almost literally masturbatory. One evening in 1930, as he was struggling to recapture the feverish spirit that had fueled his first book, Look Homeward, Angel, *Wolfe decided to give up on an uninspired hour of work and get undressed for bed. But, standing naked at his hotel-room window, Wolfe found that his weariness had suddenly evaporated and that he was eager to write again. Returning to the table, he wrote until dawn with, he recalled, "amazing speed, ease, and sureness." Looking back, Wolfe tried to figure out what had prompted the sudden change—and realized that, at the window,* **he had been unconsciously fondling his genitals,** *a habit from childhood that, while not exactly sexual (his "penis remained limp and unaroused," he noted in a letter to his editor), fostered such a "good male feeling" that it had stoked his creative energies. From then on,* **Wolfe regularly used this method to inspire his writing sessions,** *dreamily exploring his "male configurations" until "the*

sensuous elements in every domain of life became more immediate,
real, and beautiful." - Mason Currey, Daily Rituals

Remember: The first step to forming a habit is to **create triggers.**

Mason Currey's *Daily Rituals* is a fascinating look at the rituals of artists of all types. As you see in the above quote, the secret to writing every day is to tickle your balls. Sorry, females.

Kidding!

The book is fascinating, mainly because of the *variety* in rituals. Ball-tickling is the grossest, and the rituals only have one thing in common: *triggers* that induce *flow* — that feeling of getting lost in your work.

Wolfe fondles himself. Hunter S. Thompson took amphetamines. Balzac (real name) drank 50 cups of coffee a day.

Currey writes:

> As much fun as it is comparing artist's daily rituals, **the most important thing to know about a ritual is that it's your ritual.** Not Mark Twain's or Joyce Carol Oates'. It's **your energy levels, your rhythm, your daily obligations, and you should be vigilant in understanding how you operate throughout the day.** As Mark McGuinness said in Manage Your Day-to-Day: Start with the rhythm of your energy levels. Certain times of the day are especially conducive to focused creativity, thanks to circadian rhythms of arousal and mental alertness. Notice when you seem to have the most energy during the day, and dedicate those valuable periods to your most important creative work. Never book a meeting during this time if you can help it. And don't waste any of it on administrative work.

The point is: You *must* be a self-experimenter, your own personal scientist. Try things without intellectualizing them. We have a tendency to look for "scientific advice," but in realms like this, "scientific advice" tends to pretend everyone is the same, which, of course, isn't actually scientific.

Oftentimes, there is a scientific explanation for your seemingly "weird" habits, but either science hasn't proven it, or you just haven't read the right study.

Don't wait to find a study to validate what already works. Be your own study.

I could quote W.H. Auden: "Only the 'Hitlers of the world' work at night; no honest artist does."

But I write at night frequently, and genocide is my least favorite thing.

According to Duhigg, **there are five types of triggers.**

1. Time of day (we tend to have the most creative energy within 2-5 hours of waking, if that's possible for you)
2. Setting (cafe? bar? home office? work office? outside?)
3. Emotion (does anxiety make you write, and calm you down, like it does for me? or do you write when relaxed?)
4. Presence of certain people (though most people write better alone, undistracted)
5. Preceding behavior you've made ritualized (like your morning coffee)

Write down at least three triggers for your writing habit.

Be your own personal scientist.

Experiment and test your hypotheses.

Scrap what doesn't work. Do more of what does work.

Writing first thing in the morning works for lots of people. But some people can't. When you procrastinate at work, write 100 words. Just pick a time you can commit to, make an easy quota, and hit it.

And don't forget about *emotion*.

If you find yourself in a negative emotional state when trying to write, **do something that makes you feel curious, confident, or daydreamy.** I like to read, have coffee and listen to upbeat music ... because it puts me in an upbeat mood. You might want to go for a run. Listen to standup. Whatever puts you in a good mood.

My triggers are:

- as soon as I've finished my morning ritual, starting "work"
- with my first cup of coffee in front of me
- that emotion of wanting to get shit done (natural for a weirdo type-A personality like me)
- being alone, but around people who won't talk to me (cafe)
- shitty pop music on repeat (simple, catchy music helps you get in flow ... but good lyrics distract you ... so either listen to instrumental/classical, bad/catchy pop, or foreign music)

While writing, I tend to repeat the same song, endlessly, for thousands of times. This helps me ignore any lyrics, and helps create a consistent mood for each book. - Chuck Palahniuk

If you were in my head, you'd think I'm insane. But as I write this, I'm 25 minutes into a writing session. Or, play number seven of Flo Rida's masterpiece, *My House.*

Open up the champagne, pop!
  It's my house, come on, turn it up

Hear a knock on the door and the night begins

Cause we done this before so you come on in
Make yourself at my home, tell me where you been
Pour yourself something cold, baby, cheers to this

Sometimes you gotta stay in
And you know where I live
Yeah, you know what we is
Sometimes you gotta stay in, in

Welcome to my house
Baby, take control now
We can't even slow down
We don't have to go out
Welcome to my house
Play that music too loud
Show me what you do now
We don't have to go out
Welcome to my house
Welcome to my house

Morning comes and you know that you wanna stay
Close the blinds, let's pretend that the time has changed
Keep our clothes on the floor, open up champagne
Let's continue tonight, come on, celebrate

Welcome to my duck off the crib, the spot, the pad
But my house is your house if you throwin' it back
Excuse me if my home bringing the sad,
Soon as these happy faces land you can run with the cash
Home run, slam dunk, touchdown, pass
Mi casa es tu casa so it ain't no holding back

Another shot of vodka, you know what's in my glass
It's my house, just relax

[Chorus]

Welcome to my house
It's my house

Flo Rida wrote a song about the fact that he has a house, so his friends can party there instead of a bar. Genius.

Enjoy your house party, Flo Rida. I'll be getting shit done.

I used to never sit down to write. Now I can't not.

When you find something that works, do it until it stops working. Even if it seems crazy.

It's *your* ritual. If fondling yourself gets your creative juices flowing, fondle yourself.

33

Step 15: Treat Yourself Like A Baby

"The Net's interactivity gives us powerful new tools for finding information, expressing ourselves, and conversing with others. It also turns us into lab rats constantly pressing levers to get tiny pellets of social or intellectual nourishment ... **The Net is, by design, an interruption system, a machine geared for dividing attention** *... psychological research long ago proved what most of us know from experience: frequent interruptions scatter our thoughts, weaken our memory, and make us tense and anxious. " - Nicholas Carr, The Shallows*

I magine I've decided to pay you $100 an hour to write about whatever you want. Your office is a five-star, International food buffet, but you're not allowed to eat a bite during your daily, four-hour shift, and you must show up on an empty stomach. If you eat, I stab your eyeballs with chopsticks.

You have paper and pen or a typewriter. Get to work! *See spot run, spot runs so gosh darn tootin fa ...* ah, that sweet aroma of **bacon**, right next to the **pancake** station, adjacent to the best **sushi** you've ever seen, and there's **ice cream**, and **tacos** and **guacamole**, and **chocolate lava cake**, and fresh-cut **steak**, and every type of **candy**, and ...

You bite. Into everything. You're so weak.

But seriously, would you blame yourself for eating after being forced to stare at a buffet for hours?

Procrastinating while "writing" is the same, and yet we beat ourselves up when we don't produce. The way our brains are wired, and our environments constructed—procrastination is human, natural.

Especially since you're typically not being paid a dime beforehand, and nobody is watching you. Your productivity is on *you*.

When I was a full-time sports blogger, I "sat in the chair every day," as the experts tell you to do. It was my job. You "sit in the chair every day" for your job, whatever it is. And we produce, because we have to.

As soon as I quit and deadlines and paychecks removed the pressure that *I must produce*, I stopped writing for months. Despite building the habit of writing thousands of words per day, no problems, for years.

I still sat in the chair often, but I'd check Facebook and email and even read about writing, but I never actually wrote. Because while I did want to, I didn't *have to*.

Forced productivity is inevitable. Unforced production is hard.

Facebook, Snapchat, text messages, blogs, cat videos — they literally make money by *stealing and selling your attention*. Your attention is their product.

Billions of dollars are spent on distracting you. They have research departments dedicated to the science of distraction. How could you blame yourself for procrastinating?

There are *three steps* to writing productivity — contrary to what the "just sit in the chair" people preach.

1. Sit in the chair.
2. Overcome distractions.

3. Write.

Before the Internet, Hemingway and Co. could skip Step 2, mostly. Distractions existed, but they were far weaker than today's.

If Hemingway had Snapchat, he'd have sent dick pics all day and written nothing. Habit building is difficult, but overcoming distractions is even harder.

That buffet is so tempting. Want to read about politics? Watch funny videos? Talk to friends? Find a date? Watch porn? Hell, you can even do productive things. Why not read a book, or take an online course?

All of the world's entertainment and information and distraction is a click away.

You sat in the chair to *write* — and yet writing is literally the hardest thing to do, of infinite options.

Don't blame yourself for procrastinating. Would monks stay celibate if they lived inside a brothel?

I used to be hard on myself. *I'm strong enough to overcome distraction.* But like everyone, I checked Facebook and Gmail multiple times an hour.

Eventually, I realized it's not about being smart or strong. It's about being realistic — the Distraction Economy is taking advantage of the natural tendencies of human brains, and we need to take extreme measures.

The RescueTime app tracks your Internet use, and you'll be shocked at what those quick Facebook checks add up to. You're losing dozens of hours a week, and each time you shift tasks, your focus is interrupted. Researchers estimate it takes you 23 minutes and 15 seconds to recover from a tiny distraction, *each time.*

As explained in Ray F. Baumeister's *Willpower*, the founder of RescueTime, Tony Wright "was surprised to see that **nearly a third of his day was spent on what he called 'the long tail of information**

porn.' Visits to websites unrelated to his chief work. The typical visit was only a couple of minutes, but together they consumed two and a half hours a day."

Studies have shown that "people switch activities an average of every three minutes and five seconds ..."and about half the interruptions are self-inflicted."

It's just too damn easy to type "F" into your browser, hit enter, and boom, dopamine hit, distraction city.

The best writers will do anything to avoid writing. The reason the Hemingways and Bukowskis and Homers of the world didn't block the Internet was because it didn't exist. I assure you they would do it if alive today, or if not, they'd never write anything.

I felt like an idiot when I realized I had to block the Internet while writing. But then I realized I was human.

The placebo effect works even when you know you're using a placebo. It's in your mind, but it's real, and you should harness its power.

Michael Jordan famously wore his UNC shorts under his Bulls ones every game. You think he cared that's not a universal, scientific principle?

It is a universal, scientific principle that we get our best work done when we have high energy and are in a positive, flow state ... so why not do whatever it takes to trick our brains into reproducing that state regularly?

Distractions are a universal problem. Stop shaming yourself for checking Facebook, and stop acting like you can ignore the temptation. Once we accept that, we can build idiot-proof systems to overcome our natural human weaknesses.

First, build the habit.

Then, treat yourself like a bad child. Because that's basically what we are. We're innocent children in a world of irresistible temptation, and we need firm rules.

We're children being left alone in a room full of candy. Our parents tell us that candy is bad for us, that studies show each Mike & Ike reduces our lifespan by 14.69 seconds. And yet, we're gonna eat the fucking candy.

Would you get mad at a child for eating something at Willy Wonka's chocolate factory? Would you get mad at a child for acting like a child while unsupervised?

If you really don't want him to eat candy, just lock the fucking candy closet.

We need to treat ourselves like children. The only way to beat distraction is to *remove the option of being distracted*. It's the easier route, and no matter how strong we are, we'll take the easier route at least some of the time.

Fancypantses call these *forcing functions*. As Wikipedia explains, "In all modern microwaves, it is impossible to start the microwave while the door is still open. Likewise, the microwave will shut off automatically if the door is opened by the user."

We need to put child locks on the Internet aand our phones.

Neil Strauss is a prolific, talented author with a bajillion *New York Times* bestsellers. He gives his phone to his wife, forbids her of giving it to him, locks himself in a room, and uses "Indigo Family Protector" to lock himself out of the Internet for all but two hours a day when on deadline. Only his wife has the password.

You'd be amazed at how many emails you can answer in two hours when you only have two hours. Again, Parkinson's Law.

On an enlightening podcast with Tim Ferriss, Strauss and Ferriss agreed that "a writer will do anything to avoid writing."

One of the best modern authors treats himself like a four year old. You might think you don't need to get extreme, but have you written dozens of bestsellers?

If you don't force yourself to write, you won't write. Even if you love it, it's *so much easier to not write than to write.*

Treat distractions like life or death. Don't tolerate them. For emergencies, you can set your phone to do not disturb unless [mom/-girlfriend/coworker/child] calls. Tell them to only call in an emergency.

If the buffet is in front of you, you will eat. Maybe you'll fast occasionally. But most of the time, you'll eat.

Child Lock Ideas

Experiment with these. Come up with your own. Use what works, discard the rest.

Go somewhere without Internet.

1. In a perfect world, you'd go on a cabin getaway while you write your book. When you need to research something, you make a mark [rs], or keep a list of "things to research." Then you knock them out in their own separate work session when you have Internet.

Or just go to a cafe that doesn't have Wi-Fi, or a park

Leave your computer charger at home.

You'll only have a specific amount of time to get your work done, so Parkinson's Law will take over.

Work in Blocks with a Timer

Try something like the Pomodoro technique, where you work in 25/30-minute blocks, with a timer, then reward yourself with a break.

Use a program to block the Internet.

I use Self-Control. Strauss uses Indigo Family Protector and Freedom.

Phones and computers are great *tools*. You're supposed to use tools, not be used by them. As soon as your tools start using you, rein them in. You're in charge, here.

Write with pen and paper.

It seems less efficient, but that's not the case if you're less distracted. I like pen and paper for short projects, or outlining and brainstorming.

Lock your phone in a drawer, leave it at home, or put it on do not disturb in your bag, where you can't reach for it.

I once lost my phone and went three months without one while traveling. For three weeks, I constantly felt phantom vibrations and would thrust hand-to-pocket. *Was that a text? Was it her?* Then I'd realize my pocket was empty.

Notifications fuck with your brain, as *The Shallows* proves. Turn them off while you write, if not all day long.

My phone is on Do Not Disturb about 75% of the work day. There's no Self-Control app for iOS, but you can download Forest, where you set a timer and your tree dies if you check your phone. You can earn coins used to plant real-life trees.

I also deleted the Facebook app from my phone, hid the Safari app on page two in a folder, and have no apps on page one.

That's because I'm weak. So are you, unless you're an alien.

I know I'll check my phone any time I can't find the right word or get stuck. Even if I have enough willpower to resist, that simple act of not checking my phone takes up cognitive energy.

Remember: **willpower is a limited resource.** Conserve it for the decisions and productivity that matters.

Productivity is about effectiveness, not efficiency. Incremental improvements don't matter, hence seemingly irrational rules and weird routines. It's not about optimizing. It's about being realistic and experimenting and settling for good enough rather than being paralyzed by analysis.

We're all as irrational as children. Would you be mean to a child? Give yourself tough love, and lock the candy door.

34

Step 16: What Is "Writing," Anyway?

"Of all the things that can boost emotions, motivation, and perceptions during a workday, the single most important is making progress in meaningful work. And the more frequently people experience that sense of progress, the more likely they are to be creatively productive in the long run. Whether they are trying to solve a major scientific mystery or simply produce a high-quality product or service, everyday progress—even a small win—can make all the difference in how they feel and perform." - Harvard Business Review

Remember: The second step to forming a habit is to define the behavior itself, specifically.

Writing a book is overwhelming. If you "sit in the chair" everyday like the pretentious writers tell you, you'll stare at page zero of your Word Doc and cry.

"Writing" is too vague. If the activity is writing a book, have a specific intention. "Write Chapter 34, on defining behaviors." Don't combine it with other things. Don't edit while you're writing. Pick one chapter (ideally the day before, so you don't have decision fatigue before working), and focus on that one specific task.

You need to specifically define success and failure.

You need to break your writing sessions into specific, small, manageable tasks. You need to define them, and you need to know where you're at. Otherwise you'll get frustrated.

Another trick is to give yourself an easy quota to ensure regular "small wins."

Ask yourself: How many words do I think I can write every day? Cut that number in half, and shoot for it.

If you're busy and only have an hour to write, shoot for 250 words. (You'll still finish a decent-sized book in three months.) If you have two hours, shoot for 500.

You'll often beat your quota. Great! But by lowering the bar, you'll be easier on yourself, and build confidence.

You might hit an ambitious goal of 2,000 words a day for a week, but you'll probably burn out. It's hard, and demoralizing when you inevitably fail.

Adjust over time, based on your *behavior*, not your *expectations of your behavior.*

As Tim Ferriss said on his podcast, "People tend to overestimate what they can accomplish in a week, and underestimate what they can accomplish in a year."

We're bad predictors of how much we can accomplish daily. But doing a little bit every day compounds.

If you can, estimate how long it'll take you to finish your *shitty first draft* that you'll show no one. There's no pressure for it to be good. You just need to get it done. Use a reasonable length of 40,000 words (about the length of this book), and divide it by your daily quota.

You can use Jerry Seinfeld's productivity method of putting a calendar on your wall, and marking a big "X" each day you meet your quota.

That's his productivity secret to writing every day. (Plus meditating daily.)

35

Step 17: F*ck Friction

I t's essential to get rid of the friction of starting. You do this by building a habit with triggers, but there's more.

Your goal when "sitting in the chair" is to get in flow. To get the gears running. They're hard to get going. But once they do, the writing should pour out. Remove friction.

Hemingway advised to "stop when you know what is going to happen next ... you write until you come to a place where you still have your juice and know what will happen next and you stop and try to live through until the next day when you hit it again ... it is the wait until that next day that is hard to get through."

Starting is no longer a battle.

Maybe you won't use his specific tactic, but I often do. The principle is important. In martial arts, it's called "golden mean." You work hard enough to grow, but not so hard you can't train the next day.

Slow and steady writes the book.

When you're done with your writing, leave the document open and prompt yourself for what's next. Write it atop the page. Make it as easy as possible to start. Wake up, open your computer, and follow Yesterday You's instructions. Bang on the keys. Don't think.

When you hit the golden mean, take a break. *Always take breaks.*

Don't fight friction when it arises mid-work. We're taught to fight through the pain, but that's not how creativity works. You need flow. Breathe, relax, take a break, let it come back.

What you resist, persists. What you don't fight, floats away.

Your creativity gets stagnant when you sit in one place for hours. Whenever you get stuck, move. Do pushups, splash water on your face, go to a different cafe, dance like a fool.

If sitting is the new smoking, not moving is the new suicide.

I sometimes try to sit and write all day because I feel like I'm slacking otherwise. It never works. Never try to think your way out of a rut.

When your brain gets stuck, unstick your body.

Moving your body shakes up your mind.

Try the Pomodoro method (working in 25-minute blocks, then taking a five minute break). But don't stop if you're in flow. Read the book *Deep Work* for a deeper explanation on productivity.

As discussed in *Daily Rituals*, Søren Kierkegaard was famous for alternating walking and writing all day, every day. He'd get stuck, wander around Copenhagen and eventually be struck with ideas, so he'd rush home and write standing, umbrella still in hand.

As Barack Obama says, "The rest of my time will be more productive if you give me my workout time." Love him or hate him, that dude gets shit done.

Whenever you take a break, that's a perfect time for a reward to condition your habit.

36

Step 18: Treat Yo'self

"Someone who procrastinates is not irrational; it is his environment that is irrational." - Nassim Taleb, Antifragile

R emember: The third step to forming a habit is to give yourself a reward every time you succeed. Your brain is Pavlov's dog. You've earned it.

Giving yourself a reward after will help condition your brain. But you need to really enjoy it. Don't eat a piece of chocolate and call yourself a fatass. If you choose chocolate, make sure you know exactly what you'll eat (one snickers, three squares of dark chocolate), that you can enjoy *guilt-free.*

When I'm done, I workout. I like working out. If you don't, don't use this. I just finished writing, so I'm going to watch 20 minutes of standup. Bye.

OK, I'm back. I'm loose.

Play a game on your phone. Call a friend. Go for a walk. Read a book. Watch a show on Netflix. Something you actually enjoy. Enjoy it once you've done your work.

You can't *will* yourself to go to the gym, eat healthy or write *every day*. You can do it occasionally. But you can will yourself into creating a habit of doing these things effortlessly and automatically. That works long term, and it's reinforced when you reward yourself.

37

Step 19: Get Accountable

"You have to actually write. Daydreaming about the book you're going to write someday isn't writing. It's daydreaming. Open your word processor and start writing," he says. "Resist the urge to tell friends and family your story. I know it's hard because you want to talk about it and they're (sometimes) interested in hearing about it. But it satisfies your need for an audience, which diminishes your motivation to actually write it. Make a rule: The only way for anyone to ever hear about your stories is to read them." - Andy Weir

I never let anyone read my books while writing. But for my first book, I told one close friend (I was too nervous for more) that I was writing it, and for this one, I've told good friends.

By telling them I'm writing (but not giving away content), they bother me about progress. *Where is it?* I'm accountable.

One of the most powerful ways to reinforce a habit is *accountability*. Let it be known that you're writing a book and make failure have consequences.

You can:

- Use stickk.com or GoFuckingDoIt.com to make a bet. You lose money if you don't finish.

- Post on Facebook that you're doing it so people bug you.

- Tell a trusted friend to bug you.

- Give an embarrassing picture to a friend and tell him to release it if you don't hit your (realistic) goal.

- Email me at info@plat.pub with the subject "TOUGH LOVE" and I'll check in with you daily or weekly on a date you specify, once you start writing

It's *pre-commitment*, proceeding as if finishing is non-negotiable.

38

Habit Recap

"75% of America is overweight. Is that because it's so complex how to be fit and strong? Only the 1% know the answer and they hide it from you? You have to work your ass off to not hear what it takes, right? ... You're all talking about strategy, and you've forgotten psychology. Because strategy is wonderful ... but most people have strategies available, or you can get them or create them. The problem is you've got a story. Your story is why it isn't working ... If you can divorce the story of your limitation and marry the truth of your unlimited capacity, then the whole game changes. But it's hard to do that, because when you're in your story, you don't even realize that. Which is why you need a third piece ... changing people's states. Because when you're in a different state, you're a different person." - Tony Robbins, The Genius Network

That was confusing. To recap:
1) Use your limited willpower to create a habit.
2) Have triggers.

3) Test a flow routine.

4) Child-proof your writing zone.

5) Have a prompt ready when you sit down.

6) Have an easy daily quota.

7) Give yourself a reward every time you complete the habit.

8) Set stakes, accountability.

(Click HERE or email me at info@plat.pub with the subject "SUP" to receive the entire one-page guide to writing your first book, plus a list of my favorite writing books. No stories or bullshit, like in this annoying book.)

39

Step 20: STOP!

*"What you do simply proves what you believe. People will do the things that prove what they believe. The reason that person bought the iPhone in the first six hours, and stood in line for six hours, was because of what they believed about the world and how they wanted everybody to see them. They were first. **People don't buy what you do, they buy why you do it.**" - Simon Sinek*

I'm writing this book because I believe writing is a difficult, valuable skill that will increase in value in the future. That value has previously been held back by publishers' power. Not anymore. The floodgates are open, and people need to know about the opportunity.

Can you answer these questions?

- Why are you writing this book?
- What will you consider a success? (Copies sold, money made, leads gotten, subscribers gained, people's lives affected)
- What is your idea?

If nonfiction, have you filled out your "copy thesis?"

- [Any [YOUR AUDIENCE] can [SOLVE THEIR PROBLEM] by using [YOUR PRODUCT], because [HOW IT SOLVES THE PROBLEM].

If fiction:

- Have you distilled your story into one sentence that would hook a stranger? A *what if*; an *inciting incident* that drives a compelling story; or a universal theme?

Regardless:

- Did your audience respond with strong emotions in a small test? (Email, Facebook/forum/blog post?)
- Did you write all of these answers down?

Seriously, did you?
Do it.
OK.
You did it, right?
Now you can move on.
If you've written everything down.
I'll stop now.

Why don't people work hard when it's in their best interest to do so? The (short) answer is that it's really risky to work hard, because then if you fail you can no longer say that you failed because you didn't work hard. It's a form of self-protection ... Most of the psychological research on this is focused on why some kids don't study for tests. If you get drunk the night before an exam instead of studying and you fail, then the problem is that you got drunk. If you do study and you fail, the problem is that you're stupid — and stupid, for a student, is a death sentence. The point is that it is far more psychologically dangerous and difficult to prepare for a task than not to prepare. - Malcolm Gladwell

It's easy to convince yourself you're "preparing" by reading. It means nothing if you don't apply the lessons.

Write everything down.

Get to work.

You'll never be "ready," and you'll never know what's going to happen until you jump in the water. The temperature isn't changing; it's always cold, but manageable.

40

Step 21: Write Drunk

"I've had a sign over my typewriter for over 25 years now, which reads 'Don't think!' You must never think at the typewriter — you must feel. Your intellect is always buried in that feeling anyway."
– Ray Bradbury

Hemingway's famous, probably contrived quote goes: "Write drunk, edit sober." While he was a big drinker, he (actually) wrote, "My training was never to drink after dinner nor before I wrote nor while I was writing."

Regardless, writing drunk is a great philosophy.

... metaphorically, at least.

If you've written literally drunk, you've probably noticed helpful effects. It quiets The Resistance — that judging voice in your head. That's the key to writing what Anne Lamott calls the "shitty first draft," which is the prerequisite to a masterpiece.

For me and most of the other writers I know, writing is not rapturous. In fact, the only way I can get anything written at all is to write really, really shitty first drafts. - Anne Lamott, Bird by Bird

Writing metaphorically drunk is about finding *flow*.

In Find Your Creative Flow State, Jason Silva explains the neuro-science of flow. "The part of your brain responsible for self-editing literally goes dim. There's a scrambling of the self. A scrambling of the superego, that's trying to correct everything you do, and censor and filter what is otherwise subconscious. Active imagination, so to speak."

Research says we have "two complementary motivational systems: the 'thinking' system and the 'doing' system — and we're generally only capable of using one at a time."

Writing uses the "thinking system." Editing (evaluating your words) uses the "doing system."

Writing metaphorically drunk is about *not judging your words as you write*. Vomit (write) now, judge (edit) later.

Remember, the goal is to finish a "shitty first draft." You won't show it to anyone. Who cares if it sucks? You'll improve it later.

Writing a perfect first draft is impossible. Hemingway edited the end of *A Farewell to Arms* 47 times. Your nonfiction book won't need 47 edits, but it will need a few.

Projectile vomit your first draft. Clean later.

In improv, one of the first lessons is: As soon as you start thinking, you've lost your creativity.

Get out whatever is in your head.

Every human has swallowed diamonds, but eaten a ton of crap. We need to *puke everything out* so we can sift through the shit, and find the diamonds.

It's easier to sculpt shit into a sculpture than to sculpt perfectly from scratch.

If you censor yourself as you go, you're leaving diamonds inside of you. Get it all out. Write like you're an angry drunk talking to your ex. Get it all out — even the stuff you'll later regret.

Deleting later will be easy; adding diamonds from scratch will be hard. It's easier to get rid of things than add them.

The apocryphal story goes, Michaelangelo created David. A fan asked: "How in God's name could you have achieved a masterpiece like this from a crude slab of marble?"

Michaelangelo said, "It was easy. All I did was chip away everything that didn't look like David."

David is hiding in your embarrassing stories, anxieties, and poorly constructed tangents.

I personally don't drink and write, literally (it's a slippery slope), but everyone should chug a metaphorical beer and get to work.

When your goal is to puke a shitty first draft, all of a sudden finishing becomes easy and fun. Daydream on paper.

> *You finish that first awful blurting, and then you...get into your car and drive home. On the way, your mind is still knitting at the words. You think of a better way to say something, a good phrase to correct a certain problem. In short, you may be actually writing only two or three hours a day, but your mind, in one way or another, is working on twenty-four hours a day – yes, while you sleep. - John McPhee, Pulitzer-Prize-winner and author of 32 books*

Life feeds us neverending tacos filled with undercooked chicken. They're topped with shaved diamonds, but we'll never see them until all our guts are on the table.

41

Step 22: Edit Sober

"Getting stuck is the commonest trouble of all. Usually, I say, your mind gets stuck when you're trying to do too many things at one. What you have to do is try not to force words to come. That just gets you more stuck. What you have to do now is separate out the things and do them one at a time. You're trying to think of what to say and what to say first at the same time and that's too hard. So separate them out. Just make a list of all the things you want to say in any old order. Then later we'll figure out the right order ... 'I'll never get all this into one letter,' he says. He sees me laugh and frowns. I say, 'Just pick out the best things.' " - Robert Pirsig, Zen and the Art of Motorcycle Maintenence

Again, it's essential to separate writing (vomiting in flow) and editing (focused deletion, addition and reorganization). In general, editing is cleaning up puke-bits.

Assume the reader is itching to watch Netflix as they read. The second they read a superfluous word ... boom, they click on porn.

As Arthur Quiller-Couch wrote in *On the Art of Writing*, you must

"Murder your darlings."

If that word isn't better than masturbating, murder it.

Deleting your creations sucks. But remember: You needed the puke to get to the diamonds. Creativity is long and frustrating, but the work is necessary.

> *"Sometimes young writers acquire the idea from their years in school that the world is waiting to read what they've written. They get this idea because their teachers had to read their essays or term papers or dissertations.*
>
> *In the real world, no one is waiting to read what you've written.*
>
> *Sight unseen, they hate what you've written. Why? Because they might have to actually read it.*
>
> *Nobody wants to read anything ...*
>
> *It isn't that people are mean or cruel. They're just busy.*
>
> *Nobody wants to read your shit.*
>
> *What's the answer?*
>
> *1) Streamline your message. Focus it and pare it down to its simplest, clearest, easiest-to-understand form.*
>
> *2) Make its expression fun. Or sexy or interesting or scary or informative. Make it so compelling that a person would have to be crazy NOT to read it.*
>
> *3) Apply that to all forms of writing or art or commerce ...*
>
> **You learn to ask yourself with every sentence and every phrase: Is this interesting? Is it fun or challenging or inventive? Am I giving the reader enough? Is she bored? Is she following where I want to lead her?**

As Kurt Vonnegut wrote, "Every sentence must do one of two things — reveal character or advance the action." I'll add: *Will a stranger give a shit?* For every word: *Will you lose any meaning or emotion by deleting this?*

Write as succinctly as possible, but no shorter.

This book was supposed to be 500 pages. I wanted to write everything I knew about writing. I read my goals: *To give people the knowledge and encouragement needed to write a book.* I deleted more than half.

In nonfiction, every sentence must help the reader achieve his/her goals.

The other half was written to stroke my ego and impress you. That's bullshit writing. Write what you know that can help and entertain people, and nothing more.

Don't stress, though. By self-publishing, you can update your book *at any time.* Do your best, then react to feedback.

Cut the inessential, and ensure the reader can actually finish your book.

1. Vomit, no judgment.
2. Judge ruthlessly.
3. Kill your babies.

Your words aren't *actually* your babies. You don't have a Writing Vagina. They're just words, and you need to murder them. You have an unlimited supply.

It's hard, though. I paste all my deleted comment in a document titled "MAYBE LATER," in case I change my mind. It feels less permanent.

Kill your babies, but freeze their heads for later revival.

A few tips:

- Search your writing for words like "just" and "very." They're almost never necessary, and most people use them constantly. I recently edited a 30,000 word manuscript where I had used "just" 82 times.

I deleted 58 "just"s and lost no meaning.

- Watch out for sentences that start with "so," "but," or "and." They're fine in doses, but not the amount I typically use them in first drafts.
- Read your writing aloud. Literally. It's the best way to tell how your writing sounds in a reader's head. Tucker Max and Book in a Box swear by it, and so do I. Try it.
- Seriously, read your writing aloud. It sounds silly, but it's effective.
- Use Elmore Leonard's advice. "If it sounds like writing, I rewrite it."
- Take off your Fancy Pants. Be conversational.
- As Mary Karr wrote in *The Art of Memoir*, "You're better off writing fuck than copulate."

Self-edit until you've changed all your copulations to fucks.

42

Step 23: Fuck Around

"If you're remarkable, then it's likely that some people won't like you. That's part of the definition of remarkable. Nobody gets unanimous praise — ever. The best the timid can hope for is to be unnoticed. Criticism comes to those who stand out." - Seth Godin, Purple Cow

This book took me months longer than it should have. I meandered, broke my writing habits, skipped days, wrote at 9am, wrote at 3am, gave up, doubted myself, re-did outlines, stopped writing for months, told too many people about it, set my expectations too high, checked my phone constantly, and freaked the fuck out weekly.

I didn't have enough to say. I was re-hashing other books. It's not a Purple Cow. Maybe that's all true. I tried my best.

Even in writing a book on how to write a book, I struggled to follow my own advice. But I did follow it often, and it helped tremendously.

Above all, have fun, and don't put too much pressure on yourself. I regret all the days I didn't let myself enjoy the process of writing a book.

Shoot for perfection, but realize you won't come close.

43

Step 24: Give Up

"The real writer is the one that makes you feel uncomfortable." -
George Saunders

I magine your best friend is having girlfriend/boyfriend issues.
What should I do? They ask.

You went through something similar, and you have great advice.
But you're not sure you're 100% right.

I'll get back to you in a year when I've perfected my thoughts.

That's what you're doing when you wait for perfection to publish.

Your book will never be perfect, and the quicker you publish, the
quicker you can get feedback that you can implement.

You're reading Version No. 3 of this book, not including the dozens
of pre-publication edits. The first version included 14 instances of
"fart."

(Kidding. Or am I? Fart.)

You've validated that people want your book idea. But until you
publish, you don't know if you executed. You can't know if you wrote
too much, or if readers will beg for a follow-up.

Do your best, then publish and listen to feedback. Don't withhold advice that can help people. It's selfish, and risky.

I could've spent a decade writing this book. It would have been better. But the incremental improvement wouldn't help me achieve my goal of *helping people write books today.* I'd be leaving would-be-authors hanging.

Instead, I'll update the book and give readers the new versions, free.

Aim for perfection, then give up when it's "good enough" to help people. Write your next book — each subsequent book compounds the value of your previous book, because you now have two avenues to acquire customers.

Your likeliest buyers are your previous buyers, and new readers are likely to buy everything you write ... if you're good.

Quality trumps quantity, but quantity matters, too. Most people sacrifice quality for quantity, but most writers are perfectionists. Don't hide behind quality. It's admirable, but hurts your and your readers.

Again, treat your book like a startup. The first edition of your book is an MVP — minimum viable product.

Successful startups don't try to roll out the perfect product, because they don't know what people want. You can guess, but you'll be wrong. Instagram started as a Foursquare knockoff, but people loved their throwaway photo feature. Instagram listened and scrapped the unwanted features. Then they perfected what their users (readers) asked for.

You won't know what your readers want until you give them something, and watch them react.

Publish your Minimum Viable Book.

Write down the essentials — what you think your audience wants the most. Nothing more. If it goes well, you can write an expanded version of the book and give it to prior readers for free, or write a sequel.

160

As an early-20-something with little disposable income, I didn't hire an editor for the first versions of my books. Editors are fantastic, but only great ones are worth the money, and I couldn't afford them.

Get sales and feedback. Do people talk about your book? If so, hire an editor *after publishing*. Then publish a better version, and the sky is the limit.

Start with a cheap (but good enough) cover. Do people care? Invest heavily *later*. Is your book good enough to help people, and polished enough to look like a legitimate book?

Publish it and worry about perfection later.

44

Step 25: Focus On Word Of Mouth

"Every single piece of (good marketing) advice is essentially a different way to create and facilitate word of mouth. Why that strategy? Because it's the one that works best. Have you noticed I haven't written one word about book reviews or magazine interviews or radio or any of that bullshit? Because for the most part, I've found that they don't really matter. I can tell you from very extensive experience that my book has done so well ONLY because people who read it recommended it to other people, and they went out and bought it. Word of mouth. Nothing else. But here's the thing: Lasting, real word of mouth can only come from one source: Creating value. And thus leads us to the reversal ... Everything you just read about effective marketing doesn't matter...unless you have content that people like ... smart marketing only explains about 10% of my success. The most important point, the thing that trumps all the rest, is this: **CREATE AMAZING AND COMPELLING CON- TENT THAT PEOPLE LOVE AND VALUE. Everything, and I mean EVERYTHING, flows from that central principle.**

That's the thing; there is no secret to being a successful writer." - Tucker Max

People don't listen to advertising; they listen to their peers, and heroes.

Now, let me tell you about the time some dude I wrote about said he'd slit my throat.

I was one of the few sportswriters who wrote about sports betting — illegal and taboo in the U.S. My articles focused on how "experts" took advantage of the public's naivete and sold them bullshit "advice." When CNBC hired an "expert" for a new sports betting show, I had to Google him. The guy was a 3-time felon, arrested for calling the elderly and telling them, "Congratulations, you won $10,000! All you have to do is send us a $500 'deposit.' "

Shockingly, a PR director emailed me to interview him — she clearly hadn't Googled me. She was expecting a fluffy promotional article.

I gave him a chance; I asked reasonable questions. "What are your methods? What are your historical records? How do people find about you?"

He freaked out on me. *My record speaks for itself.* Cool, what is your record? *I don't keep records.* Why not? *Because I'm that good.* If you were that good, wouldn't you want to be able to cite your awesome record? *I don't need to sell people; they come to me!* But wouldn't you get even more business by keeping records?

He dodged my reasonable questions and screamed. I wrote an article about how he was "so full of shit it hurt."

He sent angry emails.

i heard your a internet wankster a pan pusher doin blogs and internet interviews out of your one bedroom apartment ... your girl probably want to suck my cock ... you probably watch star trek

Dozens of them. On they went. They were too funny not to respond, until my mother called me at 3am, terrified.

"Some guy called our house." I was renting a place, and my listed address was still my parents'.

"He said he'd 'slit your fuckin' throat, and you'd never write again.'"

My poor mother had no idea who it was, but I knew immediately. We called the police and I've ignored him since. The joke was no longer funny.

I told this story for an odd reason. It's because I believe in Seneca the Younger's stoic philosophy that, "I shall never be ashamed of citing a bad author if the line is good."

I had asked the scumbag, "How do you find clients?" He answered, "I don't. They call me."

This is a valuable marketing lesson.

Writers hate self-promotion because it's annoying. Fortunately, it's not effective, either. Word of mouth is all that matters, and the best way to facilitate word of mouth is to *give your book to those who will shout the loudest*, then sit back.

Gurus drone on about self-promotion, but that's because only the few people annoying enough to call themselves gurus can sustain years of annoying self-promotion. It's selection bias.

1. Some self-promotion is necessary. You need to get your book in front of that core audience, and they may not yet know who you are. You need to clearly articulate your book's message, so they give it a chance.

Again, the only long-term marketing that works is word of mouth. Other tactics are fine, but only when they fuel long-term sharing.

The prerequisite to marketing tactics is *writing good shit people want to talk about*. Books that make people sound and look smart. Books that make people money. Books that make people laugh, so readers can enable their friends' laughter. Books that lose people weight so their friends ask, *how?*

For nonfiction, generally: help people achieve their goals (and entertain them/keep them hooked) and they will talk about you.

Here's Grandma Bookseller's Marketing Pie Recipe:

1. Write great shit.
2. Make sure it *looks like* good shit. (Ensure them you're not full of shit, by making your book look professional and displaying social proof and/or credentials.)
3. Find your core audience (the people who want/need your book most.).
4. Get the book in their hands (give it away, and clearly articulate why they *must* read it).
5. Incentivize people to talk (give them a gift if they share your book).
6. Write more books and link to your others at the end.

Gurus preach about "big launches," but they're a lot of work, and typically sell a few books that first week ... and then people realize the book sucks, and move on. Nobody buys.

Everyone wants to do everything but the hardest thing. The hardest thing about book marketing is writing a good book, and most people don't have the cojones to do it.

We'll spend $1,000 on weight-loss supplements, but never cut down on sugar or beer. We'll buy $1,000 worth of Facebook ads, but never get vulnerable with our writing.

We value "hard work," but we measure "hard work" as "time or money spent." Bullshit. Only effort applied in the right place — to the biggest levers — matters.

Working hard on shit that doesn't matters will just make you feel a bit better when you inevitably fail. *It was bad luck; I tried my best.*

Worked 18-hour days on your customized cat litter mugs? *The economy sucks.* Ran an hour a day (but ate 4,000 calories of shit) and couldn't lose weight? *My metabolism sucks.* Bought your girlfriend a fancy necklace (but wouldn't connect emotionally)? *She's a bitch and I have the worst luck.*

It's understandable. I've done it. It feels better when we blame other people or things.

What if you prepared better?

What if you thought about how to apply your effort most effectively, beforehand, even though it was difficult?

You're reading this book, so *you* get it, unlike most.

First, commit to writing a good book. Then worry about tactics, so your book can reach its initial, critical mass. Not everyone recommends books, so you need to reach enough people to get the gears moving. Then, it can spread organically.

But if your book sucks, everything else you do is a waste of time.

Simple Rules discusses how Jim Harbaugh's strength and conditioning coach at Stanford de-emphasized weight-room numbers (bench press, etc.), and focused on injury prevention above all.

Stanford was "weak" by conventional standards, but it turned out, on-field performance was much more linked to health than weight-room strength. And his players rarely got hurt. He focused on mobility and "functional strength," and turned Stanford into a dynasty.

If you work hard on the wrong things, you shrug and say *I did all I could.*

It's true. You couldn't have done *more.*

But you could have done things differently.

You might have even gotten more out of less effort, because it was applied in the right spot.

Focus on the *outcome* that matters.

What's that, for you? Book sales? Leads for your business?

Focus on optimizing for *that*.

As Greg McKeown writes in *Essentialism*, "Essentialism isn't about getting more things done, it's about getting the right things done."

45

Step 26: Put In The Batteries

"Startups take off because the founders make them take off. There may be a handful that just grew by themselves, but usually it takes some sort of push to get them going. A good metaphor would be the cranks that car engines had before they got electric starters. Once the engine was going, it would keep going, but there was a separate and laborious process to get it going." - Paul Graham

Making good shit people want to talk about is 90% of the battle.

But if you build (write) it, they won't necessarily come (read). There are two more components, and they're essential. If people can't find your book, they can't talk about it. You have to get initial traction.

1. Install your car's engine.
2. Floor it for the first mile.

Or in non-analogy terms:

1. Make sure your book is word-of-mouth-friendly.
2. Get it in front of your small, core audience.

As Ryan Holiday explains in *Growth Hacker Marketing*:

> Outward facing marketing and PR efforts need to be targeted at a small group of highly interested, loyal, and fanatical users. Remember, most of the times we're trying to hit a few hundred or a thousand key people – not millions. Not a blowout grand opening, but a strategic opening or a stunt that catches the attention of our core audience.

Holiday tells the story of Uber, a $3 billion-dollar company that started from nothing.

CEO Travis Kalanick found a spot where his most-fanatical early adopters would be — the SXSW conference, a tech-geek hub — and gave away free rides to his core audience. Obviously, this is a losing proposition, short term. But if his product was good, which it is, he'd gain customers for life. They'd not only talk about it with their real-life friends, they'd also blog and Tweet and Product Hunt and reddit about it. That's virality. He planted one seed, and then the seed planted itself in many other avenues, to the point that my grandmother once told me, "I use the Uber."

Word of mouth is all about people signaling things to other people. You want your book title to inspire and motivate the right people to talk about it, because it lets them signal the right things to their friends. - Tucker Max

First, you have to look the part. As I've explained, there *is* a stigma about self-published books. The solution is to make your book look professional, so that most people won't even know the difference, and the others won't care.

That means you need:

1. A professional, eye-grabbing, creative cover.
2. A catchy, descriptive title.
3. A persuasive book description. (Think of it as a sales page. *How would you pitch your book to a mildly interested, skeptical stranger? Remember: They are assuming you're full of shit. You're a stranger asking for money.*
4. Social proof. (Get 25+ positive reviews, and ideally a blurb/testimonial from someone with credibility markers.)
5. A professional author page/bio, with honest credibility markers. (Mention anywhere you've been published, who you've worked for, or any noteworthy testimonials. Be honest, but come from a position of strength.)

Your book's package has to signal the awesomeness that lurks inside. The first Oreo buyer wouldn't have bought it out of a brown paper bag at the supermarket. The world would have missed out, but nobody would have known what they had missed.

Your book is a tasty Oreo; make sure you optimize the packaging. If the packaging is scammy, unprofessional or haphazard — nobody will take a taste.

46

Step 27: Follow The Sexy Book Recipe

"Openness, which encompasses aesthetic appreciation, imagination, and tolerance of others' viewpoints, is a good predictor of creativity." - Michael Pollan, The Trip Treatment

s we just discussed, your book needs a quality title, cover, book description ... and editing.

How to Pick the Perfect Title

First, read Tucker Max's Guide to Picking the Perfect Book Title for Book in a Box. Here's a summary.

> *A good title* won't *make your book do well. But a bad title will almost certainly* prevent *it from doing well.*
>
> *Based on loads of empirical research and our decades of experience in the book business, we have a pretty clear picture of what happens in the mind of a potential reader when evaluating a book.* **They consider these pieces of information about a**

book, in this order (assuming they come across it randomly in a bookstore or browsing on the internet):

The title of the book

The cover of the book

The back cover copy (the book description copy, if it's online)

The flap copy (or the reviews, if it's online)

The author bio (depending on where it is)

The book text itself (or they use the "see inside" function to read a few paragraphs)

The price

*The title is the first thing the reader sees or hears about your book—even before the cover in most cases—and **getting your title right is possibly the most important single book marketing decision you'll make** (even though most people don't think about it as marketing).*

The iconic example of the importance of a book title is the title change that led to an obscure book becoming a #1 best-seller. In 1982 Naura Hayden released a book called "Astro-Logical Love." It bombed ... She then took the exact same book, changed a small amount of the content, and re-issued it with a different title, " How to Satisfy a Woman Every Time…and Have Her Beg for More!"… That book became a massive cultural phenomenon and #1 best-seller. Same book, same content, just a different title." - Tucker Max, Picking the Perfect Book Title

Max says your title must be:

1. Attention-grabbing.
2. Memorable.
3. Informative (gives idea of what book is about).

4. Easy to say.

5. Not embarrassing or problematic for someone to say aloud to their friends.

Brainstorm a bevy of titles, in *write drunk* fashion. Don't censor yourself. Then narrow down to the best.

And don't forget, if you're writing a nonfiction book, you'll almost certainly want a *descriptive subtitle.*

There are no *rules*, necessarily, but good guidelines are:

1) Attention-grabbing, memorable *title.*

2) Descriptive subtitle (that describes benefits of reading the book).

Next, *test.*

Humans are horrible at guessing what other humans will respond to. That's why data exists. Test a few potential titles with your audience (your email list), or if you don't have one, you can use a service like PickFu, but you'll have to pay (~$300 to test four titles, only worth it if you have a big audience). You can also mock up covers and test them using Facebook ads. Which ad was clicked on most? (Keep all other variables constant.)

You can also survey Facebook friends, or people in a Facebook group like "Pat's First Kindle Book", started by entrepreneur and author Pat Flynn.

Testing is essential.

Good Title Examples

- *The Miracle Morning: The Not-So-Obvious Secret Guaranteed to Transform Your Life (Before 8AM)*
- *How Not to Die: Discover the Foods Scientifically Proven to Prevent and Reverse Disease*

How to Get a Good Book Cover for Cheap

A good cover is essential. But as we've discussed before, you shouldn't invest money in your book until you know it's a worthwhile investment. If you don't have a big audience, I'd suggest one of two options:

1. Use Fiverr to make a simple, acceptable cover for $5. (You may laugh, but my first cover, which is quite attractive, was made for $5. That's because I kept it simple. I used Fiverr and selected a nice picture of a football.)
2. Use a friend or friend of a friend who needs experience. (Don't insult a professional by asking them to work for free, but there are plenty of aspiring designers out there who can't get work that will be happy to take on a side project for their portfolio. I did this with *Mein Trump*.)
3. Make it yourself with Canva. Their templates are "good enough." (But make sure you get feedback that it doesn't look like crap. That's how I created this cover, even though I have zero design skill.)

Yes, paying big money to a good designer is a smart move ... but only once you've proven your book is worth the investment. Until then, just make sure your cover is professional, for your soft launch. Then, invest heavily.

Start super-cheap, then go high-end if the investment is justified. In general, paying for mediocrity is useless.

Go big or go home, as Confucius's Godfather, Vladimir Putin, once said.

For people who have a big audience, or money to spend, I'd recommend a mid-tier option. Great options are: Reedsy (directory of freelancers, large price range) 99 Designs (independent designers compete — costs $299, $499, $799 or $1,199 depending on how many submissions you'd like) and Archangel Ink ($298, but only one submission).

How to Write a Killer Book Description

Remember: It's not really a *description*; it's a *sales page*. Which means you need to use persuasive copywriting technique. (Email me at matt@mattrud.com for copywriting book suggestions; I've read all of the best.)

For now, here's the basic framework used on Madison Avenue for decades: **AIDA**.

- **Attention** - grab it.
- **Interest** - gain it through story/facts/case studies.
- **Desire** - show results/benefits.
- **Action** - lead them to action, make it easy/obvious.

Great Book Description Examples

F**k Feelings: One Shrink's Practical Advice For Managing All Life's Impossible Problems:

New York Times *Bestseller*

The only self-help book you'll ever need, from a psychiatrist and his comedy writer daughter,who will help you put aside your unrealistic wishes, stop trying to change things you can't change, and do the best with what you can control—the first steps to managing all of life's impossible problems.

Here is the cut-to-the-chase therapy session you've been looking for!

Need to stop screwing up? Want to become a more positive person?
   Do you work with an ass? Think you can rescue an addicted person?
   Looking for closure after abuse? Have you realized that your parent is an asshole?
   Feel compelled to clear your name? Hope to salvage a lost love?
   Want to get a lover to commit? Plagued by a bully?
   Afraid of ruining your kid? Ready to vent your anger?

In this brilliantly sensible and funny book, a Harvard-educated shrink and his comedy-writing daughter reveal that the real f-words in life are "feelings" and "fairness." While most self-help books are about your feelings and fulfilling your wildest dreams, F*ck Feelings will show you how to find a new kind of freedom by getting your head out of your ass and yourself onto the right path toward realistic goals and feasible results. F*ck Feelings is the last self-help book you will ever need!

The One Thing: The Surprisingly Simple Truth Behind Extraordinary Results:

The ONE Thing has made more than 275 appearances on national bestseller lists, including #1 Wall Street Journal, New York Times, and USA Today. It won 12 book awards, has been translated into 26 languages, chosen as one of the Top 5 Business Books of 2013 by Hudson's Booksellers and one of Top 30 Business Books of 2013 by Executive Book Summaries. Voted one of Top 100 Business Books of All Time on Goodreads. People are using this simple, powerful concept to focus on what matters most in their personal and work lives. Companies are helping their employees be more productive with study groups, training, and coaching. Sales teams are boosting sales. Churches are conducting classes and recommending for their members. By focusing their energy on one thing at a time people are living more rewarding lives by building their careers, strengthening their finances, losing weight and getting in shape, deepening their faith, and nurturing stronger marriages and personal relationships.

YOU WANT LESS. You want fewer distractions and less on your plate. The daily barrage of e-mails, texts, tweets, messages, and meetings distract you and stress you out. The simultaneous demands of work and family are taking a toll. And what's the cost? Second-rate work, missed deadlines, smaller paychecks, fewer promotions—and lots of stress. AND YOU WANT MORE. You want more productivity from your work. More income for a better lifestyle. You want more satisfaction from life, and more time for yourself, your family, and your friends. NOW YOU CAN HAVE BOTH—LESS AND MORE. In The ONE Thing, you'll learn to • cut through the clutter •achieve better results in less time • build momentum toward your goal • dial down the stress •overcome that overwhelmed feeling • revive your energy • stay on track • master what matters to you The ONE Thing delivers extraordinary results in every area of your life—work, personal, family, and spiritual. WHAT'S YOUR ONE THING?

Browse Amazon and study book descriptions. Notice the focus on *social proof* and *benefits*, instead of *features*. Don't include *everything*. Just include hooks. Get people to open the cover, and *then* your book can speak for itself.

Don't skimp on this. It's crucial.

How to Write an Author Bio

Treat this like a resume. Include credibility indicators (publications, awards, jobs, testimonials, etc.). Discuss results, and remember that the reader assumes you're a stranger full of shit. Ease their concern with *proof* you're not.

How to Design the Innards

People won't take you seriously if your book's interior is sloppy. This used to be hard. If you're a designer, do it yourself.

If not, use Reedsy's free book editor. You can write within the editor, or copy/paste from Word/Google Docs/Evernote/Scrivener ... and simply click "export file" when you're done.

You'll receive a perfectly formatted PDF to upload to CreateSpace for a paperback, and a .mobi file to upload to Amazon Direct Publishing for the Kindle/digital version).

How to Price Your Book

Price your Kindle book from $2.99-$9.99 unless you literally don't care at all about direct profits. (Then go for $0.99 for maximum leads.) Experiment with prices; there's no right answer. For short books, start with $2.99. For longer ones, I recommend $4.99 for a higher perceived value. For longer books, I'd start with $4.99, then go to $9.99 after getting enough sales and reviews (say, 50).

For CreateSpace, price your book higher. I'd recommend $6.99 for something less than 100 pages; $9.99 for anything else. Upgrade to $13.99 when you're at ~50 reviews.

This is all guesswork. Experiment. If your book starts selling, lower the price. You can change the price as often as you'd like; don't stress.

47

Step 28: Get Emails In Your Book!

"If you're a writer, the assimilation of important experiences almost obliges you to write about them. Writing is how you make the experience your own, how you explore what it means to you, how you come to possess it, and ultimately release it." - Michael Crichton, Travels

Always give readers a chance to leave their email with you. Never be annoying, but give them the opportunity, if they want it.

Failing to give them that option would be like meeting a girl or guy at a bar, having an amazing conversation, and not asking for their phone number. They would have given it to you, but they just met you, and will forget about you tomorrow. Give yourself a chance to build a long-term relationship.

Never miss a chance access your readers for life. If you've done everything properly, you'll gain tons of new fans via your book. Which means your book will be the first time a reader has come across you. Don't miss the chance to reel them in.

That might sound scammy. It's not. You're just offering the reader the option to join your tribe. If they like you, they'll be happy to give you their email. If they don't like you, they won't give it to you.

Don't be obnoxious. Offer something in exchange, and be clear that you'll send mainly free stuff you're writing, and occasionally an offer for something paid that they might like. Your future books or services.

In my first book, I offered a bet-tracking template. About 10% of readers signed up for my email list through my call-to-action.

Give them deleted scenes, access to an exclusive newsletter, a free course — anything related to your book that didn't fit in the book. Link to a signup sheet from an email list provider, like ConvertKit ($29/month) or MailChimp (free). (I use ConvertKit). Make a custom bit.ly link for paperback readers.

But don't be annoying and put a link here if you already had one in Chapter 38.

48

Step 29: Get Feedback

"One of the most important things about writing is that people are getting what you're intending. I listened to an interview with Ron Howard, where he was talking about how he shows his movie to tons of test audiences. And it's not so they can tell him what the vision for the movie should be in the rough cut form, but it's to find out whether his vision is landing with people. And if it's not landing, then he's not conveying it correctly, and he goes back and reworks it." - Mike Birbiglia, *The Tim Ferriss Show*When you think your book is "good enough," the next step is to give it to a small group of trusted friends/colleagues/fans.

People may not be able to tell you what to include or add, but they can show you *what's not working*. They can tell you what they got from the book, and you can then judge what you need to change, based on your vision and intention.

Get five or so people to give feedback, then implement it. If possible, get them to promise to leave reviews on launch day.

Give it to people who aren't afraid to tell you what they think, and, ideally, are part of your target audience. Try to get five or so people in your audience, plus a few trusted friends/mentors.

Don't get caught up in this. Five people is plenty. If you're waiting to publish because you want more feedback, realize that *you'll get feedback once you publish*. You can always pull the book, or update it. Publish your book once it's "good enough" for public eyes. Good enough to help or entertain one person. *Resistance* comes in many forms, and seeking unlimited feedback is one.

49

Aside: Editors

"What you're up against is the great unknown, the void of all Western thought. You need some ideas, some hypotheses. Traditional scientific method, unfortunately, has never quite gotten around to say exactly where to pick up more of these hypotheses. Traditional scientific method has always been at the very best, 20-20 hindsight. It's good for seeing where you've been. It's good for testing the truth of what you think you know, but it can't tell you where you ought to go, unless where you ought to go is a continuation of where you were going in the past. Creativity, originality, inventiveness, intuition, imagination — 'unstuckness,' in other words — are completely outside its domain." - Robert Pirsig, Zen and the Art of Motorcycle Maintenence

The same advice I had for cover designers holds for editors. Cheap-to-mid-tier ones aren't good value. Great ones are expensive, and worth it (I'd like to think I am!), but don't make sense until you know your book will make the money back.

Remember: Treat your book as a startup.

If you're a poor dude with no audience like I was, use a cheap or free cover designer for your MVP (first edition). Keep it simple.

I didn't hire an editor for my first book.

That might seem like an odd thing for a professional editor (which I am) to say. I wholeheartedly believe editors are worth their weight in gold.

Like designers, it's not worth it to pay for a mediocre editor. Get a great one or don't get one at all.

If your grammar will be distracting, though, hire a proofreader on Upwork. You can get one for about $100. Also, Amazon's computers will proofread your book when you upload it. (Though they're not perfect.)

If you have a big audience or can spend $1,000 or upwards on a quality editor, do it.

You can also find great freelance editors on Reedsy.

Remember: I'm not saying not to hire an editor, just not until you've proven it's worth it, or you can comfortably afford it. If your book fails, write another one, then hire a great editor when *that* shows signs of success.

By publishing a Minimum Viable Book and soliciting feedback from friends and readers (explicitly ask for questions/suggestions/criticism), you're crowdsourcing your editing.

As long as you're OK with putting imperfect work out there, and acknowledging it, you have nothing to lose. It will improve as you implement feedback.

50

Step 30: Soft Launch

"The principle of social proof says so: The greater the number of people who find any idea correct, the more the idea will be correct."
- Robert Cialdini, Influence

After you've implemented feedback and edited and murdered your darlings to the point where your book is *good enough* (MVP-worthy), it's time to publish.

But before you launch your book to the world and let everyone know about it, you need social proof. Because you're unproven.

If Michael Lewis launches a book, people will buy it. They already trust him. No stranger will trust *you* until you have social proof. Reviews are the ultimate signal.

To get sales, you need reviews. To get reviews, you need to sales.

To get reviews without sales, you have to give your book away for free.

To get people to read your book, even if it's free, you need social proof.

People won't waste their time reading your book unless they trust you. Even if it's free.

Start with friends, colleagues, and the most engaged readers on your email list. Send them a personal message, offering a free advance copy in exchange for a review. Express your gratitude. If they agree, make the book free using a "Kindle countdown promo," and have them leave an honest review.

Don't pressure anyone individually, but make sure enough people agree. Be clear about how essential it is.

Give your book to at least 10 (but ideally ~25) readers who will *promise to leave a review.*

After that, do what I call a *soft-launch.* I announced my first book's release on Facebook, Twitter and to my email list, offering my book for 50% off. You may even want to make it free, temporarily (use Amazon's "countdown deals"), but in my opinion, it's important to see if people are willing to pay for your book, because that's the best proof of its long-term viability.

Follow up with people when your book is out, and ask them to leave the review they promised. Give them time to read the book, and tell them they can be honest. Reward them with a sincere, personalized thank you, in the least.

Once you have 25+ reviews, you've got some social proof and will look legitimate to strangers. Then you can worry about reaching a bigger audience, who will take you more seriously.

For this book, I'm also testing a Thunderclap campaign. Basically, you can contact people and tell them to sign up for your "campaign," which means they'll share your book page on soft-launch day. I don't expect it to be a big boost, but it's low labor and worth a try. The beauty is that people only have to click once, beforehand, rather than schedule a reminder for the future.

Remember: People have better things to do than market your book, but they will help you if they like you and it's easy. Like, *click once right now* easy. They'll forget about you instantly, even if they like you.

51

Step 31: Publish Your F*cking Book

Y ou're ready.

Publishing a book is incredibly easy. Just follow these steps. It takes minutes.

1. Email friends or engaged readers offering a free book in exchange for a review on launch day. Give them a PDF copy before launch, and give them at least a couple weeks.
2. Get friends, family, past readers, your network to sign up for a Thunderclap campaign to share your book on its launch day.
3. If you haven't already, add your book into Reedsy Book Editor, by chapter. Then, export your file as both a PDF and .epub file.
4. Go on Amazon Kindle Direct Publishing, and follow instructions, uploading your .epub file (which will automatically be converted to a .mobi). Schedule a one-day (or more) "Kindle Free Book Promotion, so that your advance readers can download the book for free.
5. Refer to "How to Write a Book Description that Sells," "How to Choose The Right Category," "How to Unlock Secret Categories," and "How to Choose the Right Keywords."

6. Check your .epub file to see how it will appear on all devices. Contact Reedsy for support if there are formatting errors.

7. Go on CreateSpace, and follow instructions, uploading your book's PDF file and cover. Order a preview copy.

8. Wait for it to arrive. Check for errors. Also check the Kindle edition.

9. Set up your Amazon author page. Read: "How to Write Your Author Bio."

10. Set up your Goodreads Author Page.

11. Tell all of your Facebook, Twitter, LinkedIn, and email list fans about the book. Offer your book for free, or 50% off as a token of appreciation. Tell them why it will benefit them. Offer a sample PDF. Ask for feedback and honest reviews. Show gratitude, no pressure.

12. Get at least one blurb. Refer to "How to Get Incredible Blurbs For Your Book." If you really can't get one, use your best reader review. Make sure it's extra good, since their name won't hold value.

13. Thank Book in a Box and Kindlepreneur for writing the amazing guides you just read.

14. Set up a free website using Wordpress, or something similar, and put a sample PDF of your best chapter. Link to it if someone asks about your book.

15. Pat yourself on the back. You wrote a fucking book! You succeeded, regardless of sales.

16. Go on vacation, and don't look at sales. They're gravy.

(Note: If you have trouble with your .epub file conversion, download Calibre and convert your book to a .mobi file.)

52

Step 32: Give It Away

"(People) like being unsuccessful creators of writing. The comfort is fabulous, because the story you get to carry around with you is bulletproof. It's insulation. It's the outside world doesn't understand me, the outside world is against me, the outside world won"t give me a break. If only they would, then my genius would come out. But right now, I'm just an outsider. *And as long as you are carrying that around, you are safe. It has completely transferred all of the responsibility to someone who isn't you. So when you say to somebody — which is what I usually say to people who are nonfiction, or even fiction writers:* **Finish your first book, and then email it in a nicely-laid-out PDF to 100 people. Just give it away. If it's good, it'll get to 10,000 people, and then you'll have no trouble selling your second book.** *If it's not good, it's a good thing you gave it away, because no one was going to publish it anyway. Not one person has taken this advice. Not one. Because as long as you're carrying around your not-very-good novel and no agent will represent you, and no publisher will publish you, you're safe ... saying they're miserable*

makes them happy." - Seth Godin, The Moment Podcast

T he above could not be more true. I think it's smart to publish on Amazon with my MVP strategy, to maximize future returns (by taking advantage of Amazon SEO and social proof), but you could even use Godin's PDF strategy.

People think they need fancy marketing tactics, but this is all they need to do.

Message people personally. *Do things that don't scale.*

Message anyone that has shown interest in the past. People that have commented on your Facebook posts, emailed you, etc.

I wrote a Facebook post a year ago that got 75 likes. I messaged everyone, because they had shown interest.

Just one polite, personalized message, offering them a free copy, giving them a sample (like the excerpt on my wesbite). No pressure.

If they don't answer, leave them alone.

If I told you your book could get to 1,000 or 10,000 people, would you really care that you sacrificed a few hundred bucks in initial sales, if those people even would have bought?

Especially when you realize that if you did a good job, those 1,000 or 10,000 people will buy your next book or product, on and on until you die if you keep delivering?

Yes, giving books away to "influencers" will multiply your efforts. But it's not required, and it is difficult. You'd better know them and their audience, and ideally have established a relationship beforehand.

If your book won't help their audience, don't bother them.

If it will, tell them why, offer a sample, and mutual benefit. They owe you nothing, but you might be able to help them help their readers, which is their job. Empathize, as usual.

Don't ask someone to do something for you if you've never met them.

Do not cold email someone asking to *get* something.

Absolutely cold email someone *giving them a gift*.

But make sure you know them well enough (through research) to know they'll want the gift.

Make sure the gift solves a problem they have, or their audience has.

Show them you know them. Compliment them. If they have a product or book or business, show them you've supported them in the past. Be honest.

Be a fucking human.

But find other people's audiences whom you'd like to reach, and *if they knew who you were, would want you to reach them.* It's a two-way street.

Then just give your book away. It's a peace offering. You're reaching out an olive branch for a hopefully-lifelong, reciprocal relationship.

Use something like this example email from Charlie Hoehn, author of *Play It Away: A Workaholic's Cure for Anxiety.*

> ***Email to: Influencer I've never met***
>
> *Hi [author I admire],*
>
> *I'm the author of the book* **Play It Away: A Workaholic's Cure for Anxiety***. The reason I'm emailing is because I'm an enormous fan of your writing, and I would love to give you a copy of my book. It's based on a popular article I wrote about play, called How I Cured My Anxiety (#2 search result on Google for "cure anxiety," underneath Oprah.com). The article has already helped more than 100,000 anxiety sufferers rediscover the importance of play, and I'm hoping my book will help many more.*
>
> ***Email to: Loose Connection***
>
> *Hey [nice person that I like but don't know well]- My first book is coming out next month, and I'd love to send it your way. Not asking for any favors, don't worry — this is a free gift. I*

think you'll like it because I talk about managing anxiety and workaholism with play.

Would you prefer Kindle or a PDF of my *book? Just let me know and I'll be happy to send it to you.*

If not, no hard feelings — I appreciate you taking the time to read this email, and for sharing such a helpful message with the world :)

All the best,

Charlie

Important inclusions:

- Praising the recipient personally and thoughtfully.
- Establishing credibility.
- Making it easy for the other person to act. (Crucial! People have better things to do than work hard to help Internet strangers. They might want to help, but you've made them click too many times and think too much.)

Remember: Most people don't read books.

Only a handful of my friends have read my books. Hundreds have said they would. Most people don't read books. They're busy and overworked. That's fine. Don't expect people to. But also realize, you need to give your book away to people who will actually read it, otherwise word of mouth won't happen.

I'm using Godin's strategy to market this book. I'll share results with my email list when ready (email matt@mattrud.com with the subject "SUP" to be added).

53

Step 33: Anti-Launch

"One of the most common types of advice we give at Y Combinator is to do things that don't scale. A lot of would-be founders believe that startups either take off or don't. You build something, make it available, and if you've made a better mousetrap, people beat a path to your door as promised. Or they don't, in which case the market must not exist ...

I should mention one sort of initial tactic that usually doesn't work: the Big Launch. I occasionally meet founders who seem to believe startups are projectiles rather than powered aircraft, and that they'll make it big if and only if they're launched with sufficient initial velocity. They want to launch simultaneously in 8 different publications, with embargoes. And on a tuesday, of course, since they read somewhere that's the optimum day to launch something.

It's easy to see how little launches matter. Think of some successful startups. How many of their launches do you remember? All you need from a launch is some initial core of users. How well you're doing a few months later will depend more on how happy *you made those users than how many there were of them. [*

So why do founders think launches matter? A combination of solipsism and laziness. They think what they're building is so great that everyone who hears about it will immediately sign up. Plus it would be so much less work if you could get users merely by broadcasting your existence, rather than recruiting them one at a time. But even if what you're building really is great, getting users will always be a gradual process—partly because great things are usually also novel, but mainly because users have other things to think about." - Paul Graham

E very book marketing book and article praises the *big launch*, this idealized release of your book that comes with a barrage of media attention. Blogs, articles, TV, radio, podcasts. You're everywhere.

There's nothing wrong with a launch, but it takes a ton of effort (you'll probably want to hire someone), and it isn't necessarily effective, relative to time and money spent.

Remember: The essential things are engineering word of mouth, and getting your book to its core audience.

Getting featured on blogs and podcasts is absolutely worth pursuing, and you should read articles like Hoehn's "How to Hit #1 on Amazon," and Sean Ogle's "How to Guest Post," for advice.

But remember what that asshole who threatened to kill me said: "My clients call me."

If you truly have a long-term focus on quality, people will contact you to be featured on their blogs. It may be worth some effort to pitch to people, to accelerate the process.

But for this book, I decided to do a *soft launch* — the minimum effort required to hit my core audience. Because my time is best spent reading and writing.

Every minute you spend "marketing" is a minute you could spend writing. And writing is a form of "marketing."

All I did was try to get on five podcasts, five blogs, five Facebook groups, and three subreddits. Plus my email list. That's it.

By all means, do more than me. If you're planning on only writing one book, that may be smart. But don't think you *have* to do traditional "marketing."

Things like "stunts" can absolutely get you attention, but that only matters if the readers in your target audience see it. Again, nailing a tiny target with personalized arrows is far more effective long-term than chucking a bunch of arrows at a massive target miles away.

Remember what Seth Godin said. "Just give it away. If it's good, it'll get to 10,000 people."

54

Step 34: Relax About FOMO

"Before he became the most brilliant and famous man in the ad business, David Ogilvy sold vacuum cleaners door to door. Because of that, he never forgot that advertising is just a slightly more scalable form of creating demand than door to door sales. But the rest of us, decades away from a world of traveling salesmen and mail order catalogs, are removed from this fundamental reality. We forget the function behind the form and miss out on new opportunities because we can't see what's in front of us. At the core, marketing is lead generation. Ads drive awareness...to drive sales. PR and publicity drive attention...to drive sales. Social media drives communication...to drive sales. Marketing, too many people forget, is not an end unto itself. It is simply getting customers. And by the transitive property, anything that gets customers is marketing." - Ryan Holiday

Emperor Caveat has something to tell you.

This book was written mainly for first-time authors. The reason I'm so anti-big-launch is that when you aren't an established writer, your biggest obstacle is **getting stuff out there**, so that you can get feedback, practice more, and get better.

Ideally, you'll get a Minimum Viable Book out, it'll do well, you'll make it better, and then for your second book, you'll be able to hire someone to do a big launch for you.

The point is: When your biggest obstacles are getting work out there and becoming a better writer, it isn't worth your time to do traditional marketing. It probably won't work well, and your time is better spent making better stuff.

Two more things.

1. You can always do more "marketing" later.
2. Anything that gets customers is "marketing."

That includes writing more articles and books.

Get validation that people will buy your book, as soon as possible.

Then, sure, play around with pitching to more blogs and podcasts, test a stunt that proves your book concept. Buy Facebook ads.

But don't waste time or money "marketing" until you know people are buying. And don't spend time or money "marketing" unless you have data proving it's a wise investment.

If data proves a positive ROI, keep spending until that shifts.

People tell you you need to build a platform, and they're right, but don't forget:

Your Amazon page and email list are the ultimate platforms.

Amazon gives you direct access to new customers already searching for books, a hub for them to access your rising social proof (reviews), and your email list gives you a hub to connect personally with fans.

Everything else is extra.

In a perfect world, you'd probably do something like Taylor Pearson's "Jesus Marketing." That's marvelous planning, but that sort of detail scares the shit out of me. I don't want to do it. If I can get by focusing all my effort on writing and editing, and just a bit on marketing, I will. And I have.

Focus on the big wins. Those are: writing a good book, and becoming a better writer.

All of your "marketing" options will be there tomorrow, and in three years. We're in this for the long haul. Do the minimum amount of marketing possible. Give your book away to 100 people. Watch, experiment, and move on. Everything you write feeds into each other, as long as you have a platform where people can see your best work (Amazon and a website), and a way to keep updated and interact with you (an email list).

If you see an opportunity in 10 years, take it. There's no rush. Great books are timeless.

55

Step 35: Ignore Sales

What does it mean that success is as dangerous as failure?
Whether you go up the ladder or down it, your position is shaky.
When you stand with your two feet on the ground, you will
always keep your balance.

Remember the *Tao Te Ching* passage above. Remember your goals.

Remember that you can't fail if you set proper expectations. It's just one iteration of one book, one container of words in your ever-evolving mind.

My tradition is to go on vacation after publishing, and not check my phone or sales for at least a weekend.

And, remember, this shit is supposed to be fun. You wrote a fucking book.

Fart.

56

Step 36: Fucking Enjoy It

"Suckers try to win arguments, nonsuckers try to win." - Nassim Taleb, Antifragile

That's *your* book on Amazon.

Order it. Hold it in your hands, put it in your mouth.

You fucking did it.

Someone read it, even if it's just your mom.

Many people may have read it, if you *really* followed the advice in this book.

I want to read your success stories. Email me at info@plat.pub and brag.

Well done.

Fuck "getting published."

Your book *is* published, you're on Amazon, and you're a fucking author.

57

Step 37: Move On

"Trust and attention are scarce ... Earn attention. Then gain trust (over time)." - Seth Godin, The Tim Ferriss Show

I deally, you will succeed by conventional standards. If you've followed all the steps, you have a good shot.

Which means people will do as the sports betting douchebag told me and *clients will call you*.

Which means: respond to all podcast and blog and speaking offers. Maximize the value of your asset. Put it on your resume. Mention specific sales numbers and rankings. Use it to pitch freelance gigs. Use it as a business card. Use it to get jobs.

Milk your book for all its worth.

Engage with your new readers. Email them. Go back to Steps 2-3. Engage with your readers, ask them questions. Keep reading. Keep recording the language they use, for advertising copy and future book and blog ideas. Brainstorm ways to solve their problems and entertain them. Expand to products, services, coaching, consulting or online courses *if your readers want them*.

For my first book, I responded to readers who joined my email list with:

> *"Thanks for reaching out, [NAME]! I really appreciate the kind words. [GIFT] is attached. Let me know if you have any questions.*
>
> *And if you have 30 seconds to leave an honest review of the book on Amazon and share the link with anyone who could benefit, I'd be extremely grateful. It's huge for the book's success.*
>
> *Cheers,*
>
> *Matt*

I got about 90% of my 65 reviews from that response.

It had a higher success rate than asking my friends, most of whom didn't read my book.

Remember: Your self-published book *is not set in stone.* Listen to feedback, and edit accordingly if necessary.

Done is better than perfect, but done, then eventually perfect is best.

Oh, and if you could take 30 seconds to review *this* book ... I'll love you forever.

Remember: If I can write a book, you sure as shit can. Good luck, friend, and thanks for reading. Even if you don't review, I love you anyway.

Learn More

Remember: It's your fucking book. You can write any fucking thing you want. You can end with a *haifuckingku*.

> *that shit you've been through,*
> *laugh, but thank and realize*
> *your shit makes you, you*

To receive all of this info in a succinct workbook (to make taking action easier), email info@plat.pub with the subject, "AUTHOR."

You'll also get any book or product I release for a serious discount, because you're sexy.

I'll be sharing regular updates on writing, reading, researching, note-taking, writing, and all of my learnings and failures as I try to survive as a writer.

And check out my publishing company website and newsletter. Follow me on Twitter.

Remember: This was a Minimum Viable Nook. There might be mispelngs. It's not perfect, and it will surely be updated. You can receive Kindle updates automatically, but I'll notify people on my email list as well, and send paperback buyers updated copies for free.

If you have any questions, or even want to call me mean names because you think I suck, don't hesitate to email me at info@plat.pub. I want to hear from you, and will read every email.

I *love* hearing from people who actually finish books. You're rare.

Reach out.

Let's write your f*cking book.

Made in the USA
Monee, IL
26 December 2022

23485043R00118